Freedom in Solidarity
My Experiences in the May 1968 Uprising

Freedom in Solidarity
My Experiences in the May 1968 Uprising

Kadour Naïmi

Translated by David Porter

AK PRESS

AK Press dedicates this book to
the memory of David Porter
(1939–2018)

AK Press   AK Press
370 Ryan Ave. #100   33 Tower St.
Chico, CA 95973   Edinburgh EH6 7BN
USA   Scotland
www.akpress.org   www.akuk.com
akpress@akpress.org   ak@akedin.demon.co.uk

The above addresses would be delighted to provide you with the latest AK
Press distribution catalog, which features books, pamphlets, zines, and
stylish apparel published and/or distributed by AK Press. Alternatively, visit
our websites for the complete catalog, latest news, and secure ordering.

Cover design by Crisis
Printed in the USA

CONTENTS

Preface

When I was young, reading accounts of persons who had fought for freedom and solidarity was quite invaluable. They encouraged my enthusiasm to act in the same way, clarified my ideas, provided me with guides for practical action, and allowed me to form relations with people who shared the same ideals for joint action.

This is what convinced me of the usefulness of presenting my own personal account.

Included are facts of history, as they happened, for a particular young person during a grassroots social movement. This person is not a "revolutionary" but simply a student, interested in participating in social change to improve his own existence. As well, this student originated from Algeria, in what is called the Third World. Thus are linked the problem of national liberation and a different sort of social liberation. The text explains why and how that convergence occurred.

Beyond this, the social movement evoked is original: it concerns the grassroots revolt of May–June 1968 in France. The account allows one to observe the aspects of this uprising that enacted the unending historical process of humanity toward its liberation from economic exploitation, political domination, and psychological alienation.

Finally, this text shows how exceptional social phenomena of great scale, on the one hand, and the daily and ordinary existence of individuals, on the other, became interconnected.

In the end, the basic question remains: what seeds were left by the May–June movement in France? The response belongs to those who still believe in a society of freedom in solidarity.

The gestation for the birth of "my" months of May–June 1968 lasted several years. My personal case demonstrates that the movement that marked this period was not a simple chance "explosion" of "youths" without great significance. My account, of course, is a recollection from fifty years later. I tried to be as faithful as possible to what happened. However, the language I use here is not exactly the same that I would have used at the time, when quite young and with less education and experience.

Foreword

In a 1999 survey among French anarchists, the events of May June 1968 in France were ranked alongside the Paris Commune, Ukraine's Makhnovist revolution, and the Spanish revolution of the mid-1930s as one of the key anarchist events in contemporary European history. While anarchists and antiauthoritarians are those most inspired by that insurgency, large numbers of others and French society generally were deeply changed by the militant actions, critiques, and passions of that period.

For a few weeks, French workers carried out the largest wildcat strike in history. At the height of this period, some ten million (one-fifth of the population) were on strike, and workers typically occupied workplaces to prevent further activity. Many bosses were locked inside, and some workers began discussing resumed production through their own self-management. University and lycée students throughout France took to the streets, often setting up barricades against the police, then occupied campuses for weeks as autonomous zones of freedom. As the author well describes, in these contexts suppressed social desire finally gained release; free and passionate thinking and relationships quickly emerged. Many existing social barriers and privileges were simply ignored. A new, truly utopian society seemed at hand for millions as daily life and consciousness drastically shifted from a vertical to a horizontal focus. Even after the forced retreat a few weeks later, the unleashed passion and militant commitment among large numbers had liberating effects in the next decades, leading them to confront and subvert traditional relations of domination toward women, queers, students, prisoners, psychiatric patients, and others, as well as toward nature itself.

In many respects, the impact and legacy of May 1968 were comparable to those of the 1960s in the United States, but the French experience was unique in its condensed intensity on so many fronts. To remember the full impact of the time is to acknowledge that, quite unexpectedly, underlying volcanic social forces can suddenly discover vulnerable cracks in the system through which to surge forth and transform society. Continued fear of such forces and the system's vulnerability require elites to distort and denounce the true nature of that explosion.

The account in this book is unique. While French-language books on the event continue to appear, especially in decennial anniversary years, new literature in English has dwindled. Thus, the present account can educate and inspire a new generation of English-language readers previously unexposed to this critical social rupture.

This account also accomplishes a rare linkage of the dynamics of "national" and "social" liberation. The author, Kadour Naïmi, is Algerian. In his early twenties, in 1966, he came to France to study, just four years after Algeria gained national independence following 130 years of French colonial rule and a painful eight-year guerrilla war. Not only does Naïmi recall his personal participation in dangerous anticolonial demonstrations, he also links Algerian and French upheavals through the notorious French general Massu, the leader of violent, torturing repression in the Battle of Algiers and the savior of de Gaulle's conservative French regime in 1968. While the author rejected Algeria's postindependence military dictatorship, he equally wished the overthrow of French capitalist "democracy" in 1968. Nevertheless, in Algeria of the early 1960s, Naïmi was quite inspired by the massive workers' self-management movement, involving hundreds of thousands of workers, that emerged spontaneously in farm, factory, and commercial units throughout the newly independent country following the exodus of European bosses and managers immediately after the war. Self-management on this scale was found historically only in Russia of 1905 and

1917 and in revolutionary Spain of the mid-1930s. Encouraged by this example, Naïmi easily and enthusiastically embraced the self-management principle put forward in many dimensions of the May 1968 upheaval in France.

The author also repeatedly and rightfully relates the French movement to "Third World" revolutions beyond Algeria—in Cuba, China, Vietnam, and elsewhere. He learned and was inspired by the U.S. Black Freedom movement, from Italian student revolts, and from U.S. and Japanese movements against the war in Vietnam. Quite consciously, he and his comrades at the time placed the French revolt in this broad internationalist perspective.

Naïmi recollects with a first-person voice his youthful direct participation in the French upheaval and easily conveys the nature of his personal observations, relationships, elations, and eventual disappointments in the process. He does not provide an orthodox historical account, though critical events of these two months are highlighted. Instead, Naïmi's grassroots vantage point allows readers to clearly understand how each new stage of the process felt and was analyzed by anonymous participants at the base. This well-articulated personal experience invites readers to imagine themselves in the dynamic revolutionary contexts.

Finally, the account is framed by Naïmi's anarchist orientation. As he acknowledges and explains, this was not his political self-identity at the time, despite strong antiauthoritarian beliefs and his inspiration by the principle of self-management. The anarchism he critiques in his account is the individualist variety, not the tradition of social anarchism that was unknown to him at the time. Yet that absence of explicit anarchist ideological background helps readers understand Naïmi's movement in that direction as the events of May–June 1968 unfolded. In fact, this same process characterized the experience of many thousands of non-anarchist participants who, because of what they felt, observed, and lived through, were subsequently attracted to anarchism. The number of self-identified French anarchists in May 1968 was quite small, yet the spirit and insights of anarchism rapidly proliferated throughout the country, as symbolized by the ubiquitous presence of black flags along with the revolutionary red. This deep and intense exposure of millions in France to anarchist themes truly left a revolutionary impact on French culture, politics, and individual lives for generations up to the present. As the author of this book concludes, "The spirit of May lives on." Despite extensive propaganda for five decades by political and cultural forces hostile to that generalized insurrection, the liberatory spirit and ideals behind it will not and cannot disappear.

David Porter
January 2018
Author of *Eyes to the South: French Anarchists and Algeria*

I

A Pamphlet Illuminates the Poverty of Life

In November 1966, I was in my
second month as a student in stage direction at the École Supérieure
d'Art Dramatique of Strasbourg.

One day, I found myself in the meal line at the student restaurant. Someone offered me a free pamphlet. I took it and read the title: *On the Poverty of Student Life, A Consideration of Its Economic, Political, Psychological, Sexual, and Especially Intellectual Aspects, with a Modest Proposal for Doing Away with It*. Oh la!

I learned that the publication of this text was a real scandal.

Several months earlier, I had been pleased to know that a group of anarchist-tending students had gotten themselves elected to the leadership of the AFGES (General Federal Association of Strasbourg Students). This was the equivalent of the local section of UNEF (National Union of French Students). Their program? To dissolve that organization serving the authoritarian state in favor of a self-managed movement of university students.

And here was the result, the pamphlet, and what content!

Written by members of the Situationist International and students of the local UNEF section, the text was published using money provided by the university to the student organization to better "supervise" the herd—an excellent example of a good "diversion" of public funds.

Immediately, my head filled with enthusiasm. How could it not when reading these first lines of the text: "It is pretty safe to say that the student is the most universally despised creature in France, apart from the policemen and the priest."

Despised! . . . How much I suffered! How much I suffered from that at the time!

I was a twenty-one-year-old Algerian, scarcely arrived from a country where I was colonized and had taken my modest role in the struggle against the abominable colonial system. I had participated in grassroots demonstrations for independence, risking police and especially military repression. Sometimes they fired live bullets to "pacify" and "civilize" us.

I came to Strasbourg to study theater art. But also to enlarge my intellectual horizon in order to free myself from every form of ideological alienation and social servitude. And thus this pamphlet in my hand interested me to the greatest degree.

In the evening, having returned to my "housemaid's" attic room (my very modest finances forced me there), I threw myself into reading the text. The content perfectly reflected the title. I searched for this sort of intellectual nourishment. I needed it. The words I read opened my mind, thirsty for a large and exciting panorama of knowledge about society and myself. It relieved me of the depressing view of the city cathedral from my attic window. By its architecture, its central location, and its height, I saw the symbol of class domination, shown by the alienation of those it ruled.

Thus the magnificent pamphlet was welcome! . . . It remained for me to know how to make what I liked come true. Through this, I learned of the Situationists' existence. Below my eyes were others of their texts.

Later, I became aware of a work by Raoul Vaneigem, *Treatise on Living for the Use of the Young Generation.* I studied it carefully, sustained by the pleasure of discovering its ideas, totally new to me, refreshing, and highly stimulating. The artist in me equally appreciated the brilliance of its writing.

2
"It Is Right to Rebel"

Quite rapidly, I don't remember how, I joined up with a small circle of "Marxist-Leninists." That's how the Maoist tendency was labeled.

Here is why I rejected other choices.[1] I didn't appreciate the Trotskyists. On the one hand, Leon Trotsky's trajectory had not convinced me of his truly revolutionary nature. On the other hand, I thought, rightly or wrongly, that the militants of that tendency were too much the products of the socially privileged and that they demonstrated this, more or less unconsciously, in their behavior. To me, they seemed too "aristocratic," haughty, almost contemptuous.

As for the anarchists, they impressed me as quite sympathetic but limited by two faults. To begin with, I found them totally "chaotic." I was not a lover of organization, but I didn't distrust it to the extent of declaring it not useful or even reactionary. I favored organization, but when self-managed with solidarity in a free and egalitarian manner (no "leaders").

I also thought that those who called themselves anarchist were too individualistic, if not exclusively so. They shocked me by their negligence and indifference, if not disdain, toward the social dimension of the struggle—indispensable solidarity with the most destitute, oppressed, and exploited. These anarchists as well, in

1. At that time, I was unaware of two major facts: the massacres ordered by Lenin, as government leader, and executed by Trotsky, as leader of the "Red Army," against the partisans of Kronstadt soviets (1921) and those of Ukraine (1921–1922) led by Nestor Makhno. I discovered these crimes long after, especially by reading *The Unknown Revolution* by Voline. If I had known these facts in 1968, my political choice would have been different.

their own way, showed attitudes recalling those of the Trotskyists: too "aristocratic."

The "communists" of the party using that label, as well as the "socialists"—seeing their leaders and their cadres (what a word!)—I considered to be mere backups for the ruling bourgeoisie, wolves dressed like good grandmothers among the flocks of sheep. They were hypocritical lackeys and opportunists. For the rank and file, I felt pity. Their genuine good intentions were manipulated to serve opposite interests. Every chance that I had, I encouraged them to open their eyes. I think this never happened, but some of them may have ended up understanding who their real friends were.

I now can explain my motivations for the political choice I adopted.

I believed that the Chinese "Great Proletarian Cultural Revolution" was launched by Mao Zedong to prevent the transformation of the "socialism" underway in that country into a state capitalism, as in the USSR, and also to deepen the revolution in favor of the Chinese workers and to extend it to the whole world.

I thought that the prestigious Chinese leader was totally confident that the young would assist him toward that goal. "One is right to revolt," he declared. The young should criticize the opportunistic deviations of adults, including and especially those who enjoyed a revolutionary past. This was a splendid and exciting perspective for me as an adolescent. I wanted to confront every form of injustice. Those responsible were older, among them ex-revolutionary fighters who had become, once in power, authoritarian exploiters in the shape of state capitalism, as then existed in the USSR and Algeria.

Without knowing it at the time, I believed in and practiced a form of Maoism influenced by an *anarchist* vision. It gave primacy to grassroots citizens in liberating action and not to the "leaders," the "professionals" of politics and revolution, or the "avant-garde" parties.

This anarchist side came from two sources. One resulted from reading various texts: the famous Situationist pamphlet already mentioned, plus other writings of the same tendency. To my great regret, I had read nothing from other authors such as Proudhon, Bakunin, Malatesta, Voline, and so on. However, I had heard them spoken of more than once. Why did I ignore them? My dogmatism as a parroting Marxist. I had read in the works of Marx, Engels, and Lenin that anarchists were "petit bourgeois counterrevolutionaries." And there you have it! No need to interest myself in them since my "gurus" had said so. Nevertheless, my practice itself was closer to the anarchists.

And here is the practical existential cause, the second source of my anarchist tendency. In Algeria, immediately after independence in 1962 and up until 1965, I was directly acquainted with self-management. I frequently visited the shoe factory where my father was a worker. After the French owner fled, the workers spontaneously continued production on their own. I discovered with immense pleasure how those nearly or wholly illiterate workers succeeded in producing not only as before but better yet and in ideal conditions of cooperative solidarity.

In fact, from Marxism I took only what concerned theory of social and intellectual liberation. I found this in the earliest writings of Marx, those designated as "economic and philosophical," and in the text concerning the 1871 Paris Commune. These texts reflected a councilist tendency, giving priority to the action of workers rather than political parties.

In other words, I was not convinced of the political vision, especially "Leninist," that put emphasis on the "Leader," the "Supreme Savior," the progressive "intellectuals" (from the bourgeoisie) presiding over the party of the "proletariat" that needed to take power in order to establish the "dictatorship" of the same proletariat, under the inflexible and centralist direction of a single party that was "infallible" because "scientifically" socialist.

What I knew about states claiming themselves as Marxist-Leninist led me to doubt totally the value of that vision. The *nomenklatura* of these countries and their state capitalism demonstrated this for those not blinded by their own prejudice.[2] In this group of nations, I did not include China because it seemed to me that, justifiably, the Cultural Revolution denounced and fought against the pro-capitalist deviation.

---

2. *Nomenklatura*: The elite class of bureaucrats and managers.

Certain Situationist writings allowed me to understand better the failures of Marxism-Leninism and offered me a more coherent concept of social liberation. They answered my aspirations: (1) the individual was not forgotten or totally submerged by a reductive and controlling "collective," and (2) a genuine social transformation could only be radical, thus eliminating every form of oppression, whatever its justification, such as "defense of the proletariat," of the "people," and so forth.

I was not and would not consider myself a Situationist. With several exceptions, such as the November 1967 pamphlet entitled *On the Poverty of Student Life*, the work by Vaneigem, *Treatise on Living* (though sometimes marked by worthless precocious declamations), and several articles in the Situationist magazine, I found the Situationists' style, especially that of Guy Debord, off-putting, affected, pretentious, and impractical. I had the impression that the authors were daddy's boys, modern aristocrats studying people like insects while wishing to impress readers and overwhelm them with intentionally complicated and monotonous phrases. Their manner of writing compelled me to think of the *Précieuses ridicules* with its expressions such as "conversational commodities" to indicate a chair.[3]

However, I remained quite sensitive to their analysis and denunciation of every form of dominating ideology, promoted especially by the media. I forced myself to extract from their work the essential content, while removing all the "pretentiousness" of *Femmes savantes*.[4] It uselessly complicated their intentions. I had no need to admire the style of an author, to erect him as an icon. I simply searched for ideas about making practical, within the society where I lived, my ideal of *freedom in solidarity*.

To the contrary, I found the language of Mao Zedong to be clear, simple, direct, and practical: exploitation, domination, social classes, peasants, class struggle, the nature of power, demands of revolution, violence, the importance of "arms," daily struggle, the

3. *Précieuses ridicules: The Affected Ladies*, a comedy of manners, was written by French playwright Molière in the mid-seventeenth century.
4. Molière's comedy *The Learned Ladies* was written a few years after *The Affected Ladies*.

need to research before speaking (especially among the oppressed), the importance of links between intellectuals and workers. Everything was methodically expressed.

On this subject, I much appreciated the little red book of Mao. I thought it was a very good and useful summary like *Pensées*.[5] It did not generalize, like the work of Pascal or La Rochefoucauld,[6] but provided tangible reflections on the action needed to establish a just society with solidarity. The short phrases represented the quintessence of revolutionary thought and action. As well, they encouraged me to read the works to which they referred. Thus, I deepened my knowledge.

This is why I considered myself a Maoist. However, I repeat, that vision was influenced by and applied in a rather anarchist manner.[7]

My concepts and my behavior, of course, contained contradictions. I lived them as complementary riches, intended and understood according to my social objectives. I managed to integrate the need for both individual and collective liberation, in a dialectical relationship between the two dimensions. To simplify matters, I should say that I belonged to what then was called, amusingly but significantly, "Mao Spontex." I proclaimed myself Maoist while giving priority to the *spontaneity* of the exploited "masses" and to the correctness of their actions by comparison with those of the "revolutionary" parties.

---

5. *Thoughts*, by French philosopher Blaise Pascal, appeared in the mid-eighteenth century.

6. The Duc de La Rochefoucauld wrote a well-known and influential book of maxims in the early seventeenth century.

7. At the time, as I said, I was ignorant about the armed repression by Lenin and Trotsky against genuine soviet organisms (the Kronstadt commune in 1921 and the Ukrainian soviets from 1918 to 1922). I was familiar only with Lenin's appropriate work, *State and Revolution*, and his slogan of "All power to the soviets." I thought I had found the anarchist option in Leninist thought there. In reality, it was political *opportunism*, aiming to transform the soviets to submit to his own dictatorship, though masked as that of the proletariat. This illusion concerning an anarchist tendency in Lenin was my error, due to my inadequate knowledge of history.

3
Seeds

From November 1966 to the very end of April 1968, apart from my theatrical studies, certain other activities explain my path leading to the movement of May–June 1968.

I was an activist within the Strasbourg "Grassroots Vietnam Committee" working to make palpable our solidarity with the Vietnamese people in their resistance against U.S. aggression. With this aim, some among us, including me, proposed to the Vietnamese comrade we contacted that we go to South Vietnam to fight as internationalist volunteers.

Quite touched, he smiled graciously and responded simply: "I thank you very warmly for your generous offer. But, happily, the Vietnamese people are successfully resisting as they should. Your action is needed here, where you live, to show your support and to make the population here aware of the liberation struggle."

At the same time, in the "Marxist-Leninist circle," I carried on with my studies of the military and philosophical works of Mao. I was especially moved by the work entitled *Four Essays on Philosophy*. It comprised four short but dense texts: (1) "On Practice: On the Relation between Knowledge and Practice—Between Knowing and Doing," (2) "On Contradiction," (3) "On the Correct Handling of Contradictions among the People," and (4) "Where Do Correct Ideas Come From?"

However, I turned down the invitation to become a member of the UJC(ML), the Union of Young Communists (Marxist-Leninist). My mind refused to submit to any direct authority, even one sharing my ideology. In what the "leaders" referred to as "discipline," I saw a subtle but genuine servitude.

As far as I was concerned, it was enough to make real Mao's "directives" that corresponded to the practice of the UJC(ML): "Go to the people" and "Serve the people."

I participated in visits to the factory gates to "raise the consciousness" of workers about the need for the coming "proletarian" revolution, in France and throughout the world.

But, contrary to UJC(ML) instructions, I did not "place" myself definitively within the factory. I was the son of a worker, and, during school vacations, I regularly brought lunch to my father at the shoe factory where he worked in Oran. I sometimes, for whole days, spent time with him or chatting with his comrades. I was sufficiently acquainted with work conditions and the exploitation of workers. They deeply outraged me. As a result, it seemed in my case that "placement" in the factory wasn't necessary for eliminating my petit bourgeois condition and mentality.[1]

To be specific, I was persuaded that a student movement, even the most powerful in the world, could transform itself into a revolution (that is, radically rupturing with the capitalist-imperialist system to establish a different one, free and with solidarity) only by allying itself with the workers, especially those in the factories. They constituted the economic foundation of the system in place; they were responsible for production, thus for the surplus value of the investors, the diabolical "heart" of the system.

Before going to the factories, I was seized with anxiety. What will be the attitude of *French* workers toward me? And among them, potential *pieds-noirs* who angrily and bitterly left Algeria?[2] The war had ended scarcely six years earlier. Thus, would they greet me with hostility, declaring: "What the hell are you doing here, you, the *basané*?[3] Do you think you can come here to teach us a lesson? Fuck things up here? Our problems don't concern you!

1. Beginning in 1967, at the instigation of the Maoist organizations, the placement movement caused hundreds of student militants to enter the factories.

2. *Pieds-noirs*: European colonists and their descendants in Algeria.

3. Originally, this French slang term signified a person with tanned or dark skin. Eventually, it became a racist term to designate persons of darker skin color.

Go away! Go back to your village if you don't want a punch in the mouth!"

Luckily, none of this took place. I was greeted in the same way as my French comrades, with curiosity and sympathy. Curiosity to see us, students, the "privileged ones," the future "bosses" and "managers" of the business. And sympathy because we presented ourselves with great modesty, even in our clothes, not to "give a lesson" to the workers but to learn from them instead.

This sincerely humble attitude gained the expected result, especially among the oldest. The youngest ones somewhat distrusted us, perhaps fed by more or less conscious envy. They had suffered too much indifference and cruelty from those of privilege to easily believe in our solidarity—us with our delicate hands, who had the privilege to spare ourselves from "dirty factory work."

As for the immigrant workers, especially Algerians and North Africans more generally, they received me warmly. "Finally!" they said. "One of our compatriots, luckier than us, deigning to come to get to know us! . . . *Marhaba! Marhaba!* [Welcome! Welcome!]"

But not every worker would speak with us spontaneously about their difficult work conditions and their subsistence wages. I had the impression that, feeling shame, for their own dignity they refused to present themselves as complaining victims.

We had to use all our efforts to gain from them the desired information. It was still more difficult and delicate for us to explain to them the need to struggle for their liberation, within and outside of the trade unions, to convince them of the need to unify their combat with our own—we, the students, the "intellectuals," the system's "privileged ones." More than once, our declaration that we were "at their service" brought their smiles or laughs in disbelief. I understood that reaction. For people who had only experienced contempt or indifference from the well-off, how could they believe such generosity from the children of the privileged?

While it was relatively easy to speak with workers of our own age, we were much more embarrassed to address individuals who could be our fathers or mothers. Despite all our efforts, our behavior risked appearing to them as trying to teach them how to think. Weren't we "those who know" since we went to the university?

We easily imagined what workers thought of us: "But what do these privileged youths know about real life? The misery brought by the hellish factories? With never enough pay? . . . Let them first come and share our rotten existence, the permanent noise, the dust everywhere, the obligation to put up with the hellish pace while having the *garde-chiourme* on our backs,[4] the need to ask for and await permission to take a piss, the prohibition of a union or the union representative who wouldn't listen, the media that accuses us of being lazy, the metro riders who move away from us because of the sweat from our work that stinks up our clothes, arriving so exhausted at our lodging that we can only throw ourselves into bed so we can get up very early the next day, and, once again, a day of slavery, bound to a machine. Only then, when students suffer our situation in their own lives, could we speak together—for them to understand us, and for us to believe in unity."

We knew all that perfectly well. From then on, we mainly insisted that we had come to learn from these modern-day damned, to genuinely inform ourselves, and to offer our solidarity. That was true. We were totally conscious of one fact: though we possessed book learning, workers had the practical experience of economic exploitation and social enslavement directly and cruelly suffered.

We concerned ourselves especially with one specific task: to create solidarity between French and immigrant workers. The bosses, wanting to divide the working class, treated native workers better than foreigners. The latter thus somewhat resented their French comrades who were apt to profit from their small advantage. A classic opposition between the more and less miserable: war among the poor to profit the rich.

We thus had to find a way to assist both categories of workers, thereby going beyond their material division to unite them. We understood how best to fulfill this mission: the French student comrades concerned themselves with the native workers, and we, the immigrant students, were responsible for those coming from our countries.

---

4. In French, *garde-chiourme* is an idiomatic expression designating a prison guard. But it also has a slang use, meaning a foreman who watches the workers.

Given the pleasant wind of solidarity during that period, our effort to bring together the two categories of workers proved generally fruitful. An anonymous poster quite wisely made this clear.[5]

Ah! I was so happy! Happy to find myself among the salt of the earth, the lifeblood of social life, the world of the proletarians! . . . Under their modest clothes—and this is not at all rhetorical—there beat generous hearts. Despite large calloused hands deformed by the brutal nature of machine work, the mind remained sharp if one

5. "United: French – Immigrants."

permitted it. The social egoism of "each for oneself" gave way to a deep desire for cooperation. The manual worker and intellectual approached each other with reciprocal pleasure and profit. A magnificent dream, with our eyes open! Each time, at dawn and dusk, these moments of entering and exiting capitalist slavery.

These activities of study and propaganda brought religious enthusiasm as we thirsted to share the ideal of justice with those around us. Sometimes I met Christian comrades who also hung out with the workers to "raise their consciousness." At the time, I thought, "In the name of a compassionate God or simply of humanity, it doesn't matter. The essential thing is to change this world for the better."

Another fact deeply affected me. For economic and ideological reasons, I worked as a laborer during the summer of 1967 in the Strasbourg Kronenbourg beer factory. Very hard work. In a very narrow room, poorly lit and gloomy, while suffocating from heat and dust, I emptied sacks of hops into an oven.

I came to know the workers better, French as well as immigrant: their work conditions, their thoughts, their alienations, and their hopes. I came to know the ferocity of the foremen as well. They tried to draw the most sweat they could from each of us to maximize surplus value for the stockholders. However, I didn't hate these despots. I pitied them. I knew they, like us, came from impoverished families, and I understood how much their ferocious surveillance of us was forced by their superiors. Slaves receiving a wage to compel other slaves to produce the most, for the benefit of unknown masters, the stockholders. I don't know why, but each time I was at the factory or thought about it, images of slavery, like in movies, appeared in my mind. They were in black and white, certainly to maximize the stark suffering of the voluntarily condemned.

I was very happy to "go to the people" and to "serve" them, according to the Maoist formulas. My practice was consistent with my theory. They complemented each other harmoniously. I learned from both books and concrete action—the best school that exists.

I remembered the popular Algerian proverb: "Only the one who sits on the fire is aware of it." I observed that nothing was more valuable than one's own personal experience. This physical immersion, this confrontation with reality, made my ideas clearer, more credible, and more effective. Yes, indeed, practice proves the value of theory, and the latter clarifies the former.

In this way, I made my intellectual choice more practical. At the same time, in my practical engagement among the workers, I honored my own worker father. I owed him in part for the knowledge I came to possess. He helped me reflect on my own condition as one dominated and exploited. Consequently, I used my knowledge to serve those from the class of my father who gave me my life and protected me. It was a question of debt.

This consciousness allowed me to appreciate in a special way a particular category of companions. Though coming from well-off families, as part of the affluent class, they rejoined the camp of the exploited to contribute to their social emancipation. For some of them, this engagement cost them a total rupture from their families. On the other hand, they found another family, a better one: its bonds coming from free choice and genuine solidarity, in the most beautiful sense of the word.

One of these comrades became a close friend. He was an Alsatian of very pale skin, very blond hair, and very blue eyes, tall and thin in stature, with a very mellow personality and quite modest behavior. Given that he hung out with a group of Haitian students, most with black skin, these latter affectionately gave him the nickname "Nigro." His real name was Jean. Unhappily, I'm not able to recall his typically Alsatian family name.

This comrade perfectly embodied self-sacrifice, completely and without gain. I observed, I sensed, that in this he found all the pleasure he wished. I was overcome with admiration. I had never viewed so much generosity combined with such simplicity.

Not one time did I have a negative sense about the differences that distinguished us physically, ethnically, or socio-economically. I always had the impression that we were brothers, in the most poetic sense of the term.

A psychology student, he gave the rest of his time to reading books on revolution. Like me, he was a Maoist Spontex. In other words, he was down-to-earth, totally devoted to others, especially the most needy.

During group discussions, he listened a lot, very attentively. He intervened quite rarely and always with good reason. Never one word too many. When we broke out laughing at a joke, he was content to offer a charming, tender smile.

He possessed a car, a white Renault 4L. Of course, it was always available for whatever militant activity, including simply a friendly one, at day or night, at whatever location. In addition, Jean paid for gas without ever asking for or accepting money on our part. Conscious of benefiting from a family background clearly more affluent than ours, he put it to the service of solidarity.

Another fact to note: in October 1967, I went to retrieve my girlfriend in Rome where she was studying to be a nurse. Once there, I used the occasion to make contact with students I knew to be involved in protests. I visited the principal university. Students were occupying it.

What a beautiful surprise! . . . Posters everywhere and of all sorts. They supported or called for a revolt for justice within the university and in society. I noticed posters that showed the portrait of Mao Zedong. Though understanding very little Italian, I went to general assemblies and group meetings.

The movement was limited to students and to the university context. However, political groups were active within and outside of that institution. Defining themselves as "extraparliamentary," they fought the ruling "Christian Democrat" class as well as its "critically supportive" "communist" party.

I met several comrades from these contesting parties. By chance, some of them spoke adequate French. They explained to me the nature of their actions, their motives, and their goals—to contribute to a radical change in Italy, that is, to establish socialism, but the *genuine* variety. This meant abolishing the exploitation-domination-alienation social system in favor of a society of freedom and egalitarian cooperation, according to the principle of "from each according to their abilities, to each according to their needs."

Thus, I discovered internationalism in action, the consciousness that a radical change requires the engagement of the largest possible number of citizens on the whole planet. But I also noted the power of the adversaries. On the one hand, the world capitalist and imperialist bourgeoisie; on the other hand, the state capitalist nomenklatura of the Eastern bloc, led by the USSR, that controlled the majority of "communist" parties in other countries of the world.

One common interest united these two adversaries: to keep their privileges that had been derived from holding state power. To this end, they both opposed radical change—that is, change that would eliminate every such illegitimate gain, whether in the name of "parliamentary democracy" or the "proletariat."

Nevertheless, we still hoped for a possible outcome. Two facts motivated us.

First, some among us hoped that the Chinese Cultural Revolution might genuinely deepen world revolutionary action. The risk of conflict between the United States and China was possible, but we were not afraid of this. At the least, we would escape from the impasse decreed by "peaceful coexistence." And the Vietnamese people would not remain alone to experience U.S. aggression. Second, in the mountains of Bolivia, Che Guevara had created a *foco* (focal point) of anti-capitalist and anti-imperialist struggle. We knew that leaders of the USSR and the local Bolivian "communist" party were hostile toward it. Its leader, Che Guevara, had launched the appeal to "Create Others, Ten, a Hundred Vietnams." We hoped to see other centers of armed resistance surge forth in other Latin American countries, the "backyard" of U.S. imperialism.

It was in Rome that I learned some of the saddest news of my life, the assassination of Che Guevara in Bolivia by a native agent of the CIA. In violation of official rules for conflicts of war, the captured prisoner was executed in summary fashion. His enemies assumed they could deny the crime by hiding the place of his burial.

They committed an error in allowing his body to be photographed; the image traveled around the world. What a stirring resemblance between his still body and that of Christ! Nearly the same age, a bare torso where the black holes from bullet wounds could be seen, closed eyes, shaggy black beard, the troubled facial expression. Those who distributed the photo thought it would dissuade others from following his example. To the contrary, they made him an icon calling for revolt.

The most remarkable is this: I did not feel that a leader, a chief, had died, but rather a simple militant, a simple combatant, a friend.

I recall certain of his declarations that touched me the deepest. He said, citing the Cuban poet José Marti: "Every true man ought to feel on his own cheek the blow given to the cheek of any man." He had said, "If you tremble with indignation at every injustice, then you are a comrade of mine."

His letter to Fidel Castro explained his reason for renouncing every state position, every privilege, to pursue popular liberation struggles. What a letter! What words! What absolutely overwhelming generosity, especially to read at my young age. We had our secular and revolutionary "saint."

Che was only thirty-nine years old. When still young, more or less at my (our) age, he had renounced an ordinary and lucrative medical career. He preferred to fight, despite his asthma, carrying a gun, against dictatorship, and not even in his country of birth but with companions of another Latin American nation, the island of Cuba.

With victory achieved, he quickly renounced a privileged post at the center of a new state regime. He went to pursue, in another country, the fight for the liberation of oppressed peoples.

Many of us strongly aspired to imitate "Che" in one manner or another.

In Strasbourg, my attic room was among several identical chambers that formed a sort of apartment. We lived there as a community. Aside from myself, the others were Haitian comrades, all students, all Marxist-Leninist Maoists. Once finished with their studies, they planned to return to their country to join in clandestine activism to overthrow the Duvalier dictatorship.[6] Most of them were at the faculty of medicine and planned to serve as doctors or nurses in the future guerrilla war.

At the same time, they pursued their political education and perhaps also a practical training, especially in handling weapons. Of this last aspect, I knew nothing. Of course, I was seen as only an

6. That of doctor François Duvalier, nicknamed "Papa Doc," who began his rule in 1957.

Algerian comrade, destined to return to my country of origin, to act in the same way as the Haitian companions in their nation.

The failure of the Bolivian guerrilla struggle, although quite painful, did not totally surprise me. I knew that this attempt had too many enemies. On the one hand, the U.S. imperialists and their native lackeys; on the other hand, and most gravely, the nomenklatura of the USSR and that of the Bolivian "communist" party.

We knew that the leaders of the latter failed to provide needed logistical support to the guerrillas. The campaign was seen as too inopportune, contrary to the choice of "peaceful coexistence."

Sad was my return to Strasbourg.

4

There's Warmth in the Air

Like many of my comrades, I was attentive to what was happening in the world. Very encouraging signs came from everywhere. We needed to understand what was happening and how we could integrate it.

I already mentioned Vietnam, Cuba, and Bolivia.

Other events gathered all my interest. With my comrades, we knew about them from the press and television. We discussed them at length and ardently at every opportune moment: meals at the student restaurant, nearby cafés, walks, study groups, and activism.

These were the events that caught our greatest attention and from which we sought to draw lessons for ourselves. The admirable and imposing civil rights movement of Black citizens, led by Reverend Martin Luther King, was an excellent lesson of grassroots and nonviolent struggle against a system that was democratic only for some, to the detriment of others.

On U.S. university campuses, students resisted their government's aggression against the Vietnamese people.

On January 5, 1968, winter was lit up by the Prague Spring. Contesting ferocious domination by the state nomenklatura, this grassroots and nonviolent movement sought a genuine citizens' democracy. We were reminded of the proletarian revolts in Berlin (1953) and Hungary (1956). We were happy to learn that the Bolshevik ideological freeze had been challenged once again by the proletariat itself. They spoke of "democratic socialism," of "socialism with a human face."

On January 19, in Japan, Zengakuren demonstrators undertook the most spectacular action, an example that circled the globe. They marched against the USS *Enterprise* aircraft carrier. Thus, I learned the nature of their organization. This Japanese federation of autonomous student associations, created in 1948, evolved from groups with quite limited syndicalist objectives, protecting student rights, into organizations intervening in the political arena from extreme left positions.

The demonstration against the U.S. naval ship was justified by the fact that the United States used Japan as an operational base for their infamous, disgusting, and criminal aggression in Vietnam.

On television we watched the student action in Tokyo. It was perfectly organized: compact ranks, helmets, and self-defense staves. The police set up a barricade. A frightful clash between adversaries ensued. The protestors reached the dock of the aircraft carrier. They explained the nature of their demonstration, then invited the sailors to disobedience. Following this was a march toward the Ministry of Foreign Affairs. The students reached it and went inside.

We were amazed, admiring, and thoughtful at the exemplary nature of this action and anxious to see how we could learn from it.

We observed enthusiastically the planet's turbulence: diverse social movements (youths, workers) and those complementing each other (national and social liberation).

Notably, in Europe (especially France and, beforehand, Italy). In Latin America: Cuba, Bolivia, Argentina, Mexico. In Eastern Europe: Czechoslovakia. In Africa: national liberation struggles (Congo and Portuguese colonies). In the United States: actions already mentioned. In Asia: Vietnamese resistance, Japanese Zengakuren, Chinese "Proletarian Cultural Revolution." In the Middle East: Palestinian resistance, at that time basically secular, against Zionist colonialism.

What a magnificent and grandiose liberating turbulence around the whole world! . . . The wretched of the earth and the slaves of hunger stood up! The rumbling volcanic crater! It had to be then the "eruption" of world revolution.

With my comrades, I assumed that hegemonic capitalism and imperialism were against the wall, everywhere. The economic "well-being" that it provided to citizens of the developed center of the world (especially, full employment, consumer items, and "leisure") were now not enough to make them complicit, contenting themselves with crumbs from the exploitation of natural resources and labor power of the "underdeveloped" world.

Our group was convinced: the ideas of freedom, justice, and solidarity were riding high. We needed to participate in the strengthening of this revolutionary storm.

I shouldn't forget the role played by songs and music in my growing sensitivity to injustice and in my determination to fight against it. The revolutionary songs of the world, in French versions: Russian, Spanish, Cuban, the Chinese "The East Is Red." From France: songs of the French Revolution, such as the joyous "Carmagnole"; of the Paris Commune, like the gentle and poignant "Le Temps des Cerises"; from the anti-Nazi Resistance, "Ami, entends-tu . . ."; the songs of Jean Ferrat, Jean Ferré, Brassens, Marc Ogeret, Jacques Brel, and so on. From the United States, the splendid and tender Joan Baez, with songs such as "We Shall Overcome," which became the hymn of demonstrations for civil rights of African American citizens.

More exemplary than the others, Joan Baez, the young, frail, and beautiful girl, with a Mexican father and Scottish mother, complemented her artistic engagement with the social: active and direct support, first, to the civil rights movement in the United States, and second, to the Vietnamese people in their resistance against imperialist U.S. aggression. This second activism cost her a month in prison. I knew that she was only four years older than me.

My heart was warmed again, my spirit encouraged, my hope reaffirmed.

I had only disgust for the stupid contortions and ridiculous lamentations of male and female singers sold as spectacle merchandise by the dominant system. They represented exactly the type of society that suffocated me.

Here is my physical appearance at that time:

The beard, as imitation, paid homage to the Latin American "barbudos" guerrillas. It also had the advantage of making me appear a bit older, thus more respectable before paternalists of every sort.

5
The Beautiful Spring Arrived!

Influenced by all the facts mentioned above, I then learned of the launching of the May movement in Paris! We received the vital information. It especially came from action by those in Paris calling themselves the Enragés.[1] What a word! . . . They chose for themselves the name of the most radical social activists in the 1789 French Revolution. In such a way, history comes from ebbs and flows, but at different levels.

Of course in Strasbourg, as in Paris, this new flow tide was opposed by shocked student organizations, supposedly of the "left," "progressive," "democratic," and "socialist"—in short, those of civility. Genuinely confrontational actions threatened their privileges as representatives or partners of the ruling system.

For me, the upsurge of the movement was not totally surprising. I said already that I was aware of the protest movement on university campuses in the United States. As well, I had observed directly the militant mobilization in Italy—in Rome and in Turin, where I briefly visited. Thus, I asked myself, "When will the movement explode in France? Isn't this the country famous for its revolutionary moments?"

Situationists and other political groups of the extreme left were also agitating among students. Some of them, including my Maoist group, were active among workers, at the factory gates. "There's warmth in the air," according to the going expression. More precisely, before the surge of the movement, it glowed. Then the fire of the movement burst forth.

---

1. In English, the "very angry ones" or "furious ones."

At Strasbourg, the mobilization was immediate. The center of protest? . . . The university—more precisely, its best symbol, the Palais Universitaire.

Of course, I was one of the occupiers. Not as a leader: I possessed neither the training, nor the capacity, nor the ambition for that. I acted as a simple militant. However, not as a member of the Marxist-Leninist group. I was a sympathizer but not officially integrated. My activity was freely given, that of a "Mao Spontex," as already mentioned.

The first basic decision was made and materialized on May 11 when we proclaimed the autonomy of the university—in other words, self-management. The majority of students and most of the teachers supported this: supposedly 6,000 of the former and 150 of the latter.

The red flag floated above the Palais Universitaire. It embellished the sky with the color of hope . . . and of the blood shed for freedom by preceding generations! Other flags, those of the anarchist black, draped the interior walls.

At the first general assembly, an enormous crowd of excited students, their hearts pounding, their spirits on fire, their faces shining with hope, actively participated in the construction of a new world, in line with our hopes for justice and mutual aid. The activism resembled what I had seen at the University of Rome.

We looked at each other, happy with this explosion of revolutionary enthusiasm. It contradicted the experts who declared that France slept. Well, some, because of daily militant action, had suddenly awakened: the university youth or, more exactly, those who refused future recruitment into the class of rulers or their slaves.

As I already said, we knew and reminded ourselves that other students like us had already begun their liberating revolt elsewhere: on the campuses of even the world's "imperialist beast," the United States. Their example encouraged us. They opposed the aggression of their army against the Vietnamese people to prevent reunification of the country and its independence. The official pretext was "to contain the spread of communism."

Reporters' images showed almost daily the high number of U.S. soldiers killed in combat in the rice fields, all of them young, including students fulfilling their military duty. Other images revealed the horror of the occupying army's violence: napalm bombings of everything living; villagers massacred, without distinction of age or sex, on suspicion of supporting the guerrillas—in other words, supporting the independence of their country. This war of aggression outraged us immensely, deeply offending our sense of justice.

And the heroic resistance—the word was not at all rhetorical—of these poor peasants inspired us but also demanded that we ourselves act, for our own account. Echoing in us was Che's appeal to create other Vietnams, other fronts of the anti-capitalist and anti-imperialist struggle.

Moreover, we feared that, in the end, the Vietnamese resistance would succumb under systematic carpet bombing, that the criminal generals of the U.S. army would return this people to what they arrogantly called "the stone age." A Hitlerian language was employed by false believers in democracy, claiming to represent "civilization" and "freedom" in the world.

It was thus important to create other centers of resistance to imperialist capitalism everywhere where action was possible. I found myself, with others, in France, in Strasbourg. We had the physical strength of our youth, its typical strength of heart and mind, and our beautiful ideal of freedom coupled with justice.

The occupation of the Palais Universitaire came about not only through beautiful protest action. It was equally important to deal with ordinary daily needs. We had to give every attention to order and cleanliness. Taking our turns, we accepted these responsibilities. We insisted that our occupation not be accused of dirtiness or disorder, even in the toilets. Our presence should reflect in everything the beautiful ideal we believed in. We took part in all this with the sense that such details embellished even more our social action.

One fact, however, saddened me. In the daily general assemblies, where the chance to express ourselves was totally free and encouraged, few girls would speak. For me, coming from an Algerian society where the female was generally relegated to domestic tasks, without the right to speak, I expected to see more female participation in a "democratic" and "civilized" France, especially within a movement dedicated to liberation in every realm, including for women.

Alas! During the general assemblies, very few female speeches and, among them, very few of note. Nevertheless, I hoped for rapid progress and to see more significant participation.

My personal sensitivity to this issue had a family origin. During my childhood, I greatly appreciated the involvement of my mother in my education and in the growth of my awareness. I thus expected, as eminently positive, female speeches in our meetings and female participation in decision-making. Hadn't Mao said that "women hold up half of the sky"?

Then came the moment when I remembered that in reality I was not a university student but a student at the École Supérieure d'Art Dramatique. I returned there to inform myself of the situation.

It was calm. No occupation, and classes continued. I quickly understood why.

The relations between us students and teachers, as well as between the students and the director, M. Pierre Lefèbvre, were cordial with mutual respect, a harmonious collaboration that would not motivate any resentment or critical action. Thus, activities went on, peacefully and enrichingly.

Even so, I would have liked artistic involvement within the movement from my companions. However, for my part, I gave priority to direct social action. That's why I didn't dwell on motivating my École companions, other than by certain hasty comments.

One piece of news saddened me. I was informed that the theatrical work that I wrote in 1967 and that the troupe at the Théatre de Levallois had planned to stage in the spring of 1968 would no longer be produced. As a result of the social events, the mayor's office had blocked the necessary funds.

Titled *Être ou ne pas être* (*To Be or Not to Be*), this work portrayed the struggle of the Vietnamese people, first against French colonialism and then against U.S. imperialism. Furthermore, in epic style, the piece sought clearly to raise the consciousness of the French public to support the Vietnamese popular resistance.[2]

Here is the ending:

2. See *Éthique et esthétique au théâtre et alentours*, book 1, http://www.kadour-naimi.com/f-ecrits_theatre.html.

"Epilogue"
(with a calm voice)
Dear spectator friends, dear comrades,
Thank you for listening and watching!
Some among you
will forget "this whole story" tomorrow!
Granted, to those,
permit me to say:
Yes! Forget this whole story!
Think only about your job,
about your little family
and about yourself!
Be afraid only for your personal self!
Think only about your money and your health
if they are good!
Yes! Make yourself a good soul with a good conscience.
Enjoy yourself or act like it, it doesn't matter!
But, get drunk! Make up some illusions!
And especially, try to quickly forget
what you have seen and heard today in this place!
As if none of this concerns you.
After all, you have enough worries, in your daily life;
and you are, thank God for you!,
far from Vietnam,
far from Asia
and from the war!
At what was modestly represented for you here,
it was, after all, only theater!
(*Hymn of the South Vietnamese Liberation Front*).

The End.

My artist's chagrin lasted for only a little while. I preferred to contribute to changing society by direct citizen action, not by theater. I thought that the best creative expression.

6

Speaking for Action

Extraordinary news filled us with joy: on May 13, throughout all of France, a general strike broke out, followed by demonstrations where students, teachers, and *workers* marched together, united!

The following day, in Paris, students and teachers of the Sorbonne proclaimed it a "free commune," and the faculty of Nanterre demanded its autonomy. We were proud, in all modesty, to have acted first. We had proclaimed the autonomy of our university on May 11.

What was essential was that things were moving the right way not only in the universities but also among the workers and throughout the country. The liberating storm had arisen!

I was happy! . . . So happy, and my companions the same. We had the sense of dreaming with our eyes open.

Finally! The moment to release every energy.

We recognized it and met together to express freely our ideas, our desires, our plan of action, and we discussed as long as necessary—that is, at length, with patience and passion, not always controlled . . . until our bodies and minds were exhausted. Sometimes without finishing all the arguments.

We had so much to say and hear and had been waiting for so long. Young people were full of ideas! For a long time suppressed, they now poured out in a magnificent waterfall, abundant, refreshing, stimulating what was needed and yearned for: liberating action!

At that point various committees emerged to plan multiple activities, to organize effectively, even for the smallest aspects of collective life.

The walls filled with posters, proposals, tracts, notifications, and even drawings (satirical and erotic), poems of known or anonymous authors, spontaneous thoughts on aspects of the reality underway. The walls spoke and exchanged proposals freely. New postings tried hard to respect the old ones that remained topical.

One source of inspiration, even for the non-Maoists, were the famous *dazibao* (handwritten, big-character wall posters) of the rebels in the Chinese Cultural Revolution.

However, and this was fundamental, all of this activity came without "higher" authority, without "gurus," but in the most free, most horizontal, most democratic manner.

This lack of hierarchy was also expressed spatially. This meant no speakers on a raised platform with listeners below, but everyone on the floor, in a circle, such as shown in the photo below of an assembly at the University of Strasbourg in May 1968.

This community arrangement was fundamental. It demonstrated and symbolized one of the essential principles of the movement: the equality of everyone. First, this was shown in a physical sense, as a prerequisite for full participation in the debates.

If a person showed the makings of a leader, it was only for the quality of his or her proposals; members of the assembly could freely demand needed clarifications in order to modify, adopt, or reject declarations of the speaker.

Each person was invited to formulate ideas. The timid were encouraged to express themselves, but without too much insistence

that might make them feel ill at ease, thus avoiding every form of authoritarianism, even when animated by good intentions. That was one of the pillars, one of the basic driving forces, of the movement: the absolute refusal, without compromise, of every form of authoritarianism, including especially that paternalism that imposed content by claiming to possess certain knowledge.

And complicated words, overly academic concepts, and stylistic speeches had no place and were totally incongruent. The simplest (not simplistic) terms and expressions, the most understandable, the most concrete, and the most practical gained the most attention and appreciation. The movement sought to reduce if not eliminate all distance, every barrier between specialists and ordinary student-citizens. We often succeeded, so great and powerful were our desire and determination.

We thus found ourselves together on the same equal footing, communicating freely to build our solidarity, with sincerity and warmth, each according to his or her abilities, all for one and one for all. The assembly represented one of the strongest moments of collective fusion, not by sheep submitting to a shepherd but by citizens consciously acting within a common movement for one unique goal: to change life for the better for each one of us, thus for all.

7

To Be the Best Activists, We Had to Study, Study More, Study Always

Our discussions and actions clarified a shortcoming among most, if not all of us: our knowledge was inadequate to change things as we collectively wished.

There were many urgent questions to resolve. How to convince the majority of students who were indifferent or hesitant? How to relate to manual and intellectual workers? How to gain the active solidarity of all those who were interested? How to confront effectively the ideas of the small conservative groups? How to avoid being victims of violent and terrorist actions committed by the small fascist groups? How to win over police officers, these children of the working class? In case of a worsening situation, how to gain the solidarity of soldiers who would otherwise be ordered to repress us?

Other questions also demanded solutions. How to establish correct relations between guys and girls, thus to avoid hearing more of the latter's justified complaints: "Hey, revolutionary males, who washes your socks?" Or to hear their reproach: "Hey, dear lover! Did you know that a woman would also like an orgasm when making love?"

So vast and total was the project at hand, every question seemed important and was linked to all the others. "Everything and now!" Many suggested making this program concrete. But when some suggested priority actions before others, whistles and groans often dissuaded them from continuing to speak. It was difficult to reason calmly and coolly when in the midst of too many people, where eager emotions dominated, especially when we'd discarded every form of authority.

Every tendency expressed itself, competing for approval by a majority: Maoist Marxist-Leninists, Trotskyists, socialists of every variety, social Catholics, Protestants, anarchists, Situationists, and so on and so forth.

Like most of the unaffiliated students, I defended the self-management option. I thus had to study to know how to act. In an educational sense, we were all more or less insufficient, even the best among us.

So, among those in the group I belonged to, every other night we didn't sleep.

Each of us used our rest time to read in the quiet of our rooms, to study with great attention and dedication: newspaper articles on current events, brochures concerning how to organize militants, essays on revolutionary tactics and strategy, books on the history of revolutions in both the Third World and metropoles.

Other nights were dedicated to meetings to discuss what we read so that we could work together to understand what wasn't clear or convincing.

One comrade really astonished us. He was a third-year history student. We admired how his face resembled that of a pre-revolutionary Russian anarchist. Because of this, in honor of Mikhail Bakunin, we affectionately named him Baku. He was characterized by his large, half-shaved, bearded face, his black eyes shining with intelligence, his modest behavior, his voice mild but firm. For him, one night was enough to read an essay of two or three hundred pages.

The next day, at our meeting, he would present a detailed summary and comments. On the manuscript pages he held with delicate hands, I noticed his writing style: thin letters, hasty, nervous, very compressed, fully filling the page. His facial expression showed feverish intensity in the process of learning and communicating his insight. Yet he stated only what was necessary, with an even tone and absolute simplicity, without affectation, never encouraging us to feel his intellectual superiority. He made me think of a splendid flower offering its fragrance naturally. What a marvelous specimen of a comrade, of a human being!

Even at the student bar, if the discussion didn't interest him, he discreetly went over to an unoccupied table, removed a book from his pocket, and plunged into reading, always with a pencil at hand for taking notes. We let him do it, knowing that when we met again, his reading would be for the gain of all of us.

Sometimes, when our brains were exhausted by intellectual effort, we relaxed by drinking beer, wine, and especially Cuban rum with cigars, for their taste and "to assist the Cuban economy." Some among us accompanied this pleasure with a game of chess or go to exercise our minds through cleverly combating the enemy.

At this time, I learned how to play the latter game, a sort of Asiatic chess. It was said to have inspired Mao Zedong in developing his tactics and strategy for revolutionary struggle. Essentially, the game consists of encircling the enemy elements, then eliminating them one by one or altogether. In contrast to the classic chess game, there is no hierarchy: no king, no queen, and no simple soldier, only identical pawns. The two adversaries differ by colors, white and black.

This process reflected two visions of the times. On the one hand, Mao Zedong demonstrated the strategy for world revolution. The "countryside" (the oppressed peoples of the "Third World") needed to encircle the "towns" (the developed countries); afterward, the latter would rejoin the revolutionary movement, especially because the developed nations no longer could access the primary resources, stolen from the world's "periphery," that had made possible their capitalist domination.

On the other hand, Che Guevara had begun the struggle in Latin America. Despite his death, revolutionary turbulence was boiling over in several other nations of the region, as well as in Africa and Asia. "A single spark can start a prairie fire," wrote Mao. He proved this with the glorious struggle of the Chinese people, culminating in the famous Long March against internal feudalism supported by foreign imperialism.

This was why the game of go interested some of us, including me.

A few words about how we acquired books. Like I said, my financial resources were extremely limited. Aside from the wages

I gained during the summer of 1967 working in the Kronenbourg beer factory, my money came solely from my work at the student restaurant. That job had the advantage of providing me free meals.

However, buying books was a real problem. Curiously, the practice of lending books to each other was rare. "A book lent is a book lost!" was the justification. I understood.

My friend Nigro himself voluntarily gave me free range of his rich library. As to the works of Mao, they were provided to me for free by my Marxist-Leninist group, which received them from an organ linked to the Chinese embassy. At the bookstore of the French "communist" party, I bought several other books. Their price was affordable, and the manager was a simple man, a militant, so nice and trusting in me that I wouldn't allow myself to take books without paying.

Yet I needed to gain others as well. The bookstores sold them at a price beyond my economic resources. Thus, I proceeded, like other comrades, with "expropriation." I stole them. And I took so many, sometimes four or five at a time, though always fearing I would be discovered. Happily, that never happened. Sometimes I carried out the operation with the complicity of another comrade who served as a lookout. Afterward, I would serve him in the same way.

Our justification for this act was simple. Knowledge is not a product to be sold for a profit. It should be free. Furthermore, capitalist bookstores set their prices to take account of a certain number being stolen. Thus, my conscience and that of my comrades were absolutely at ease. In addition, I knew a young guy, not a student, who offered to provide us with any book, whatever the value or size, at half the sale price. All we had to do was tell him the place where it was sold. In contrast to other comrades, I refused his services.

The nights devoted to educating ourselves or having fun, in line with our ideal, were the most beautiful of my life. I don't think I'm wrong to say that this was the same for my comrades. However, from time to time, the body made its demands. At night it demanded of us to stay in bed for the needed biological rest.

The reason for this "tactical retreat" was not only the energy spent for study and pleasure. We also had other activities every day: organizing and then participating in small meetings and in general assemblies; editing tracts aimed at students, at factory workers, at the general population, and so forth; printing those tracts on the mimeograph; and finally distributing the same documents while talking with those we encountered.

8

"Serve the People" and Serve Oneself

Among some of us, especially the Maoists, the theme—"serve the people"—was an absolute imperative. Several anecdotes explain this.

One evening a comrade, Edith, and I studied Mao's little red book. We had met several times before. Suddenly Edith asked me with the smoothest tone and a tender smile: "And if we make love?" I stared at her half surprised. In effect, our meetings had created affectionate feelings in each of us. This comrade was pretty, her supple and thin body pleased me, and her perfectly aligned face and clear brown eyes charmed me. The soft tone of her voice soothed me. Everything about her enchanted me. Added to this, we strongly bonded psychologically through our common ideas and shared feelings.

I responded to the smile of my comrade with pleasure, then declared: "We haven't enough time. What time we have should be used to learn and make revolution." My dear companion understood. We exchanged a second smile, that of love, then we continued to study, the heart a bit broken but the mind made up. Sacrificing ourselves for the people was our pleasure.

One Maoist comrade, Laurent, went to hand out flyers at the gates of a factory. Another militant went with him. By surprise, a fascist commando attacked them. Laurent lost an eye.

Despite this, back from the hospital as if it were nothing, he pursued his activity at the factory gates. It was not he who told us what had happened, but the comrade who accompanied him.

Laurent was a young guy, especially handsome, with a quite charming face. With painful sadness, I glanced discreetly at his eye,

45

now bandaged and not usable. Laurent maintained his same behavior. I didn't notice the least anger or hate toward his aggressors. I had the impression that, for him, militant activity had its risks, that it was quite simply normal to accept them. I sensed in him an intense fire, calmly controlled, a serene strength, a devotion as natural as breathing.

He spoke little, just with essential words, precise, simple, practical, and pronounced with modesty. I exaggerate nothing in this portrait; I describe him faithfully. Laurent incarnated a secular saint, the ideal of a social militant. His greatness came from his absolute simplicity and the tranquil anonymity of his engagement.

Such devotion deeply impressed me. He remains in my memory the most beautiful example of totally generous action, where every reward resides in the act itself.

Certainly, persons like Nigro, Baku, Laurent, and Edith had been the lifeblood preparing and undertaking the movement of May–June 1968 in Strasbourg. It's impossible for me to imagine this sort of human being becoming a turncoat, transforming engagement into a "career" in the camp of the exploiters. To the contrary, such people remain faithful their whole lives, whatever their difficulties, to the ideal born during their tender youth.

There are characters and behaviors that do not deceive, as the Italian proverb affirms: "Il bel giorno si vede dal mattino" (The beautiful day reveals itself in the morning).

I've known other militants whose future political evolution I would never guarantee. Something in their words (lacking precision), their silences (untimely), their actions (ambiguous), their gaze (elusive) caused me to expect their likely change of position, depending on the strongest wind. They are weather vanes! . . . Obviously, I avoided these people as much as possible without forgetting that they created an obstacle to overcome. In short, not everything was beautiful in the best of worlds.

One regret, a preoccupation, nagged my mind. In my study circle were only university students. No manual worker, no factory worker, no peasant. However, workers our age existed, and we knew them from our visits to the gates of the factories where they worked. I considered their absence doubly negative.

On the one hand, this failure showed us our inability to sensitize workers enough to lead them to study with us. On the other hand, this failure deprived us of the practical perspective of the persons we gathered to study.

More than once, I expressed my discontent on this matter, especially to my comrades with more training and experience. Their responses were "We're thinking about it," "We're moving in that direction," "This will come."

They spoke to me of actions meant to create committees of struggle at the workplaces, to build an autonomous workers' force opposed to the trade union bureaucracy. In the meantime, I thought with bitterness: "If, through bad luck, I'd been a worker, I would not have been able to be here, to study with my student comrades."

My contacts with workers, especially immigrant Algerians, showed me the difficulty of convincing them to come study with us. In effect, we had control of all of our time, while they devoted eight hours and more to a debilitating, exhausting job. Consequently, where could they find the strength of spirit to study with us for at least a couple hours? They first had to satisfy basic physical needs: to eat and to sleep.

And Saturday and Sunday? Hmm! Workers equally needed to recuperate after spending their energy throughout the workweek. Some devoted themselves to their partners and children. Others, immigrants without families, sought to relax at a café. I thus concluded: "A dreadful and bitter dilemma. Apparently with no solution. How, then, to carry out revolution?"

My analysis was that in Strasbourg were two general tendencies among the students. The first conceived of social change through close and complementary linkage with working people. This demanded going to them, getting to know them, exposing ideas to them, helping them to free themselves from their capitalist alienation, and convincing them of their interest in rejoining the revolutionary movement.

Maoists, Trotskyists, and left Christians were distinct in their concern to serve the people. For that category of militants, individual liberation necessarily came through liberation in the social realm, first of all for those most dominated and exploited by the capitalist system. Consequently, problems that were strictly individual, especially sexual liberation, were secondary.

To the contrary, the second tendency prioritized individual change. Each person was self-responsible and thus needed to find the personal path to liberation on his or her own. In this second movement group, the question of sexual liberation was as important as all other issues. For some, sexual liberation even came first and affected all the rest. We had here what could be called "individualist anarchism" that, I will add, gave priority to eroticism in every form, the first being to enjoy the body—beginning with sexuality.

One amusing anecdote on this subject. On certain occasions of disagreement between partisans of the collective and those privileging the individual, the latter threw out to us with friendly irony, "Go fuck and you'll be better revolutionaries!" Our reply was: "Divert your eyes from what's between your legs and you'll understand better how to change the world!"

In fact, these two conceptions of change complemented each other, more or less harmoniously. The "individualists" participated in the movement (assemblies, demonstrations, and so forth), and some "collectivists" found time to indulge in bodily pleasures.

For both basic tendencies, the movement had one goal in common: the abolition of every form of individual and social alienation in favor of a society where each one could enjoy fully his or her capacities without negating those of the others.

To complete this picture, I should note one difficulty I had as the movement went on.

In Strasbourg, there existed a small group calling itself, if my memory is right, "Zionist socialist Jews." Like the rest of my comrades, I basically disagreed with them.

These Zionists denied all rights of existence to the Palestinian people. They considered them to be part of the Arab people, who should thus go live in one of the Arab countries and leave the whole territory for the Jewish people to whom God had given the "Promised Land."

Of course, to begin with, we objected that the Palestinian people had inhabited the region labeled Palestine for a long time. Nevertheless, we understood the need for those who escaped the

Holocaust to have a territory in which to live. Thus, the region should be divided in an equitable way between the two peoples, and they should be encouraged to cooperate for the common good.

Only one member of the Zionist group was willing to discuss this issue with us. The others refused any dialogue and held themselves at a distance, openly demonstrating aggressive hostility. Their behavior reminded me of the fascists we had to deal with from time to time. "How strange they are, these human beings!" Sadly, I thought, "Children of the victims of fascists are behaving like fascists, without even knowing it!"

Among us militants was David, a Jewish comrade from the United States. Quite sympathetic, intelligent, and with a sense of humor, he had a certain eastern appearance despite his blond hair and short height. He wore glasses for near-sightedness. Even he was unable to establish dialogue with members of the Zionist group. They accused him of betraying the Jewish cause.

During the assemblies, however, the Zionists intervened, although very rarely. Their stand of denying totally the rights of the Palestinian people deprived them of much attention. The majority of those present supported the solidarity of peoples, without exception, without special prerogatives for one or the other, even when declared by Yahweh, even in the name of the Holocaust.

We called attention to the long and continuous existence of a more outrageous holocaust caused by the world capitalist-imperialist system: millions of deaths by starvation, by sickness for lack of medicine and clean conditions of life; to this were added tortures and assassinations by military dictatorships and, not to be forgotten, imperialist aggressions.

Was this not the holocaust of holocausts? Its crematorium ovens were the slums of the "Third World." No need for trains or gas or camps. The "final solution" consisted of emptying Africa, Latin America, and Asia of their "useless mouths" so that inhabitants of the "rich" and "civilized" countries could profit further from these territories' material resources. The Palestinians were part of the "surplus" population to eliminate.

David, the other comrades, and I were sad to observe the minds of these "Zionist socialists" closed to the drama of the Palestinian people. "Are you first of all socialists or Zionists?" we demanded of them. "First of all Zionists," they immediately responded.

We understood: "socialism" was solely for Jews, to the detriment of Palestinians. For the Zionists, to deny this was "anti-Semitism." Though of Semitic origin, even I was accused of the same fault, and David as well. Ah, words! Ah, bad faith! Ah, how one hides from oneself the mentality of domination!

I remained quite deceived. I could not understand how sensitivity about the tragedy of a people one belonged to could justify indifference to the tragedy of another people, a victim of the first.

Let us add a personal fact but of a different type, rather sympathetic. Within this Zionist group militated a young girl of my age. Her smiling character completely contrasted with that of her companions, and her very agreeable physical appearance charmed me. A beautiful oval face, a light brown skin, large sparkling brown eyes, her long black hair, a bit frizzled, an inviting shape. I also liked her biblical name, Sarah. It stimulated my poetic-erotic imagination. I so much desired to be her Abraham.

We had occasion more than once to let our eyes meet, quite discreetly. They spoke of our pleasure to contemplate one another, to become acquainted. . . . I sensed that without the group's control over her, we could have sympathized with and, even more, loved each other.

Alas, the beautiful one was tightly watched over. It even seemed to me that the leader of their group was possessively fixated on her. There was never occasion to find ourselves alone together. During the assemblies, her companions surrounded her. At protests, I searched for her eyes but never found them. It seemed to me that the group didn't participate in the collective street demonstrations. Perhaps my memory is wrong.

9

Spokesperson for the "Third World"

The day came I so waited for! The great day! . . . The first impressive street demonstration. It assembled the greatest number of citizens, not only the majority of students, but striking workers as well. If my memory is right, it was May 7 or May 8, but I'm not certain. The gathering took place in a large space in front of the Palais Universitaire. My heart beat quite joyfully; my spirit blew the most jubilant horn.

Let us back up. At the meeting the night before, the organizing committee assigned me to write and deliver a speech to the crowd in the name of the "Third World," before the march began. I didn't understand the reason I was chosen. The committee had two other comrade activists, a Haitian and a Congolese, with two significant advantages over me: they were several years older, and they had clearly better political training compared to my own. I knew that they were the leaders of their respective Marxist-Leninist Maoist groups.

So, why choose me to deliver the speech? The response to me was unclear. They were content to tell me, "It's better that it be you." I then quickly asked myself, "They chose me because I was the youngest?" . . . This was true, but I was the least experienced.

It is true that they listened to the text that I wrote out. They corrected it lightly, then approved it. I ended up explaining to myself the reason for their decision: to avoid putting forward the Haitian or Congolese comrades. Their double status as leaders and foreigners could provoke their arrest and expulsion from the country. To the extent that I also might be the object of such action, this was not as serious. I was only a simple militant at the base. I thus accepted the mission conferred on me, not by "submission" to my "superiors," but from awareness that it was better to risk the "sacrifice" of a militant of the base than that of a leader.

It was thus that the following morning they gave me the microphone on the front steps of the Palais Universitaire. I first had to calm and control my emotions. Here I was, at twenty-two and a half years old, an Algerian scarcely liberated from colonialism, son of a worker, much unaware in matters of revolution; here I was assigned to give a public speech, the first in my life, at Strasbourg, before an immense crowd assembled to express its wish to change France for the better and thus contribute to influencing the rest of the world.

What responsibility I had to take on! . . . The sheet containing the prepared text of my speech trembled in my hands. I couldn't wait any longer. I launched forth: "Vietnam! Cuba! Algeria! Palestine!" At this last word, someone groaned close by. I looked at him: it was a "Zionist socialist Jew." However, being in the minority, he stayed there, swallowing his bitterness.

I continued my delivery by describing and denouncing the wrongdoings and crimes of various imperialisms toward countries of the South. I evoked the diverse struggles of peoples to resist and to promote a just society of solidarity in that part of the world, while hoping as well to contribute to the same kind of change in the countries engaging in exploitation and aggression.

The end of the speech received, according to the common expression, loud and warm applause. I was quite content. Against the rulers of their own state, a mass of citizens came together in solidarity with the resistance struggles of poor peoples, victims of the injustices committed by the world's powers, including France.

Other comrades spoke. They explained the nature, motives, objectives, and justifications of the demonstration. They did their best to create the enthusiasm needed for its success.

Then came the moment to begin the march.

Then a singular event took place.

Where the "Lumpenproletarian Scum" Begin
"Storming Heaven"

In the group to lead the procession, there was some hesitation concerning who would hold and wave a red flag that had been prepared in advance.[1]

Suddenly, I saw someone seize it vigorously. He held it as high as possible and resolutely marched forward. This act was noticed by very few people. My surprise was immense and my joy infinite! . . . The one who held the symbol of the struggle was a very special friend.

Several years older than me, he lived in the house across from mine. We had finally met in the street. He was Algerian, like me. But what he wore was impeccable and intimidated me, with my working-class origin and modest clothes. Despite this, we got on well. He learned of my difficult economic condition and my strong desire nevertheless to become a playwright. These two aspects touched him.

"I'm also from a poor family, peasantry of the mountains," he claimed, "and I wanted, like you, to study a good profession. Unfortunately, I didn't have the means to attend school beyond the primary level, and didn't even finish it. Then unemployment, followed by poverty, brought me to France. Here, the injustice of bosses in my wage jobs disgusted me. What could I do then? . . . With a little money saved, I took my time. I mainly went out with girls, beautiful

1. In an oft-cited phrase, Karl Marx praised the 1871 Paris Commune as "storming heaven" in a letter to Ludwig Kugelmann on April 12, 1871. In their 1848 Communist Manifesto, Marx and Engels referred to the lumpenproletariat deridingly as the "social scum."

ones, but, like me, of the working class. My handsome appearance pleased them. One day, with money running out, I asked a 'fiancée' to give me some money to live. Unfortunately, she was in the same economic condition as I was. She then threw out jokingly: 'If you wish it, I could take to the sidewalk to gain some money!' 'Why not?' The reply came from my lips spontaneously without thinking."

This is how D* . . . became a pimp.

I sense the enemies of May 1968 crying out, scornfully sneering: "So! This then is what the movement was about! The social scum!" In turn, a spot-on Marxist-Leninist would declare, with arrogance and disgust: "What's this story about? . . . To pretend that a product of the immigrant lumpenproletariat led a grassroots French demonstration?"

Well, yes! . . . This was the reality. But, imbeciles that you are, doesn't such a movement that transformed a pimp into a fighter for social justice that will eliminate every form of pimping, including exploitation of the arms of workers and the brains of intellectuals, prove its beauty and its liberating effectiveness?

Let us add that D* had a quite particular personality. Despite his repugnant job, he maintained his sympathy for poor people, for the *déclassés*. Sometimes, money received from the "girls" assisted those less fortunate. He offered it to me many times, knowing my precarious economic situation. I always declined. He was sad about it but understood my attitude.

I persuaded myself that, deep down, he respected me more. One day, he insisted to me, sadly, because he'd drunk too much: "I would like to be like you! I admire you! You have the same origin as me, but you, you knew how to come out of it with dignity. I thank you for having consented to be my friend. I have no others."

It was this man that I saw at the gathering for the demonstration, in the group at the front. Even more, he waved the standard of proletarian revolt, and while dressed in a matching suit and tie! (The photo on the next page was taken with him, a short time before or after the demonstration. I don't precisely remember. I erased his face to respect his privacy.)

D* then proceeded to march, setting everyone in motion. Of course, I was the only one who knew his occupation. For everyone

else, his elegant clothes and his handsome physique suggested a student from an affluent and cultivated family. Only the bronzed tint of his face could have suggested immigrant status. But at this very moment, that trait had no importance, except for the pleasure of observing the absence of ethnic distinction among demonstrators.

What a miracle! A pimp had not forgotten his alienated grassroots origin. Despite exploiting persons less fortunate than himself, he maintained the instinct of revolt for a beautiful ideal, and he showed it. He knew (as he confirmed to me afterward) that his behavior risked attracting attention by the police, but he preferred to express what was the best in him on this so special occasion.

Naturally, as soon as the first red flag appeared against the blue sky, others of all sizes surged forth above the crowd, and black ones as well.

The crowd set forth.

II

A Powerful River of Freedom and Solidarity

I was added to the lead group, several rows behind the front. We were finally together, students and workers.

It's difficult to find words adequate to express my happiness at the time.

Several years earlier, in Algeria, I had marched in grassroots demonstrations demanding national independence. As the "Wretched of the Earth,"[1] we faced off against the colonial soldiers. If we had been captured, we risked imprisonment and interrogation, which inevitably meant torture.

From time to time, the military would shoot live bullets at us. By luck, I always escaped these consequences—except once. While fleeing one time, I had to jump over a barricade placed by soldiers in the street. These were made of barbed wire and held by iron rods in the shape of a cross. One of my knees hit the point of a rod, but I was able to get myself out of danger. The scar still remains.

There I was then in Strasbourg, on the soil of the former metropole ruler, to demonstrate for a higher ideal: justice and solidarity in France and the world. My comrades were mostly French, but some were from every continent, either here to study or to make a living. We were together, side by side, chanting and proclaiming our common demands.

1. Title of the influential 1961 book about the Algerian and "Third World" revolutions by militant writer Frantz Fanon.

Our ranks covered the large avenue and made a very long and imposing mass of citizens. No soldiers, only police in antiriot gear. However, our own demonstration security force channeled the march and protected us effectively. Nevertheless, we had to plan for the eventual intervention of provocateurs—from outside our ranks (fascists or police in civilian clothes) or from within (hotheads or, again, fascist or police provocateurs).

Local residents watched us from their balconies and windows. Some gave friendly smiles; others showed their solidarity with a hearty salute. Only rarely were there worried faces. And none were hostile. Perhaps they hid themselves or refused to offend their eyes by viewing the "screaming rabble," the "riffraff emerging from the sewers." We knew that the privileged part of the population feared losing their advantages. That was our goal: an equitable division of the social wealth.

Oh, it was so beautiful! Equality, freedom, fraternity achieved, lived together, with no distinction by nationality, skin color, age, sex, or social status! A unique lava of hope for a better world surged forth from the volcano made up by the best part of ourselves! Mouths exclaimed in the spring air: "Students, workers, same struggle!" "Frenchmen, immigrants, all united!" Other slogans demanded justice and solidarity.

I dreamed with my eyes open! . . . The most marvelous of dreams! . . . I was not an Algerian but a comrade among comrades; not a student, but a citizen among citizens; not a youth or a male, but a human being among other humans. Our commonality: to demand our dignity, our right to a life of freedom and solidarity.

Not long before, my feet had treaded the same Strasbourg pavement as a poor student, an ex-colonized, fearing those obsessed with dark skins, an isolated individual among a herd of similar others, indifferent if not hostile toward one another. Now I marched down this same pavement as a free man among free others, singing our desire for a society without humiliation of the majority by a minority.

The expression of "brother" and "sister" used during the time of Algerian national liberation now became "comrade" and "companion." We no longer needed a family reference to express our solidarity. We did better with terms suggesting the human collectivity all together.

In my life, two days were the most beautiful, and they continue to animate my love of life: the day of Algerian independence, July 5, 1962, and the day of that first social demonstration in Strasbourg. The world was thus moving forward in a positive direction. And I was an active agent for it, with all my physical and psychological capacity.

Though an immense mass of citizens swept forth, the demonstration proceeded with entirely no incidents, with the sympathy of that part of the population who followed us with their eyes from houses or sidewalks.

It was a great and significant citizen victory.

12

To Build the Movement, We Had to
Explain, Explain, Explain

In the following days, we needed to
find how to consolidate and enlarge the movement. Ah, the beautiful month of May! The same month lived by the Paris Commune,
almost a century earlier. We were energized by its spirit.

During our nights of study, we read and reread about achieve-
ments . . . and setbacks. We would hope for the first while avoiding
the second. All the time knowing that we lacked strategies or adequate organization.

We had to create *everything*, as *fast* as possible. Our best advantage: the "spontaneity of the masses" and their inventiveness. The
Paris Commune, Russian soviets in 1905 and 1917, Spanish collectives during the antifascist civil war—these were our references. At
the university, they were translated as self-managed student assemblies and committees, with action proposals, discussions, counter-
proposals, further discussions, and so forth.

Whoever knew the most offered knowledge to the others, but
without using this for personal benefit to direct, that is, to impose
or command. Such a wish was impossible since the collective valued
its autonomous thinking, expression, and decisions.

We examined ideas carefully, sometimes for too long and not
usefully, and hair-splitting was part of the collective dynamic. Finally,
decisions were made, by raised hands and majority votes, but without
showing contempt for the minority. Practical experience would con-
firm the justice or error of one or the other position. A new debate
would then take place at the next committee meeting or assembly.

I thus participated in the fullest form of democracy. It was so beautiful and so necessary. Of course, it demanded time, lots of it, and patience, lots of that also. These concessions guaranteed the perfect exercise of collective power, derived from each of us according to our personal capacities.

Then came the more limited meetings for writing tracts to distribute to students and to workers at factory gates. There as well was direct and total democracy. Equally long, detailed, and patient arguments led eventually to unanimity. When that proved impossible, majority decision would rule; however, this would leave us a little bitter. We would have liked to have complete agreement since we had such mutual respect at our meetings.

One day, the organizing committee at the university gave me a mission that filled me with pride and joy. In the name of this committee, I was to explain the nature, motives, and objectives of the movement to groups coming from Germany. I prepared myself to the best of my intellectual training to carry out the work by reading movement documents and books explaining the movement and revolutions in general.

I slept strictly the minimum I physically could. Each minute counted for maintaining and developing the movement. The race we were engaged in was opposed by determined and formidable enemies: representatives of the bourgeoisie and their "social democrat" allies of every persuasion. They did not hide their intense will to limit our movement, reduce it, distort it, besmirch it, and bury it.

I met the German friends and sympathizers.

What a transformation this implied! A youth, an Algerian, explaining to Germans about the May movement in France. I remembered the foreigners completely integrated into the Paris Commune of 1871. Internationalism became once again a reality; I lived it personally.

During the meetings with small groups from the other side of the border, I was pleasantly surprised to see, instead of long-haired rebellious youths, ordinary citizens, youths and adults, apparently peaceful and simply curious to learn about the reality that intrigued them. This was a good sign. The movement now was enlarging its influence to a part of the ordinary German population.

With all my zeal, I tried hard to understand my questioners, then to explain to them as well as possible what they wanted to know. Principal question: "Why are students revolting, against what and toward what end?"

To summarize, here was the substance of my responses at that time. First of all, it is not only a student movement, as certain government or private organs wanted people to believe. Certainly, students were the initiators. But later the workers joined in. The best proof was the huge demonstration that took place in the city, and the strikes underway.

Students originally revolted in Paris against the prohibition of guys visiting the girls' housing. This led to confronting the university administration. This opposition then moved on to critique reactionary and authoritarian professors. Instead of teaching objectively and scientifically, thus encouraging the development of free conscious citizens, they indoctrinated students to serve and justify the dominant social system. The mandarins produced other mandarins to satisfy the dominant caste and were compensated with a comfortable salary for services rendered. Some, the most servile, were rewarded also with "honors of the Nation." The refusal of the majority of mandarins to change their method provoked the occupation of the university symbol, the Sorbonne.

Quite rapidly, with the "plain" ready to catch fire from the slightest spark, other universities, then the lycées, the collèges, were captured by students. Even future artists transformed their "School of Fine Arts" into a "People's Workshop." There they produced masterworks absolutely surprising in their innovation. Only a creative imagination aspiring to the combined freedom of individuals and their collectives could produce such work. The posters were the most obvious and radiant examples.

Other "honorable" establishments also were captured by the students, such as the Odéon Theatre, with the blessing of the artists.

From then forward, student assemblies became the rule. The prohibition against guys visiting the girls' housing, then the authoritarian attitudes of the professors, were denounced and rejected as aspects of a socially retrograde system. Its foundation was the domination by a minority caste over the majority of citizens. The system is called capitalism, along with its logical consequence, imperialism.

We had decided to abolish this foundation in order to establish a functioning society where hierarchical authority and its consequence, social inequality, will be replaced by egalitarian cooperation in every domain of social activity.

"Then it's revolution that you want?" certain visitors asked, with more or less fear or astonishment.

"Yes, you can call it that."

I reminded them, with examples, that that aspiration characterized humanity everywhere and always. Among them, in Germany, the peasant revolts, such as those of Thomas Munzer in 1525, and the workers' councils in 1918.

Some of those speaking were astonished at my knowledge, given my youth. Were they also surprised to see, speaking to them about a French event and German history, someone who physically showed origins from an "underdeveloped" country? I didn't and couldn't know. But I would have liked them to appreciate that the desire for social justice could come from any human on earth.

Generally, at the end of the information meeting, I noticed some rather anxious expressions. Did these represent fear of a general upheaval of French society that might overflow to Germany, or, to the contrary, did they represent *hope* for its accomplishment? I didn't know and, most often, thought that I didn't need to ask. I didn't want to embarrass them, and I preferred to let them leave while hoping that they would meditate in a positive way about what they had heard.

Sometimes, however, it seemed to me necessary to understand the cause of concern in the eyes of the foreign visitors. I should not only give them information but, equally, learn from them in order to understand the impact of our movement. Each of these two aspects was important.

When I asked, our German friends gave rather vague and reserved responses. Were they afraid to give their opinions in the presence of their companions? Or, rather, did they need to reflect before expressing themselves? Some of them, especially the youngest, showed through satisfied facial expressions that they sympathized with the movement. They let us hope that once back home they would be active in creating their own resistance.

Ah! To enlarge the movement! That it could exist on the other side of the border, in the country well-known to practice, par excellence and by tradition, order and obedience. What a magnificent prospect!

13
"CRS = SS"

In the night between May 10 and May 11, in Paris, the first "night of the barricades" took place. Stunned and outraged, we saw on television the quite brutal repression of student demonstrators by what were called the "forces of order."

State violence revealed itself, shed blood.

It was rationalized by attacks on store windows and burning cars that were blamed on the demonstrators. The demonstrators denied responsibility, blaming it on provocateurs of the police itself as well as on fascist agents.

Both of the latter had reason to create an excuse for violent police repression and its justification by the public, who would be naturally outraged by "acts of wanton vandalism committed by the leftists."

Indeed, how could such destruction of private property serve the movement? We had noticed that television images showed clearly that police action was not aimed toward violent demonstrators alone. It was generalized, with no distinctions, and was even directed against passers-by and against demonstrators already on the ground and unthreatening. To beat and brutalize everyone found on the streets, until blood flowed, was a repressive and terrorizing tactic, an example of the terrorism of the state. A lesson from Machiavelli: govern by punishment and fear.

Part of the population was outraged. "What then is the nature of this regime," they asked, "that allows itself to bash young people, boys and girls, making their blood flow, with the risk of killing some of them?" Some remembered the pogrom against Algerians, in October 1961 in Paris, and the bodies thrown into the Seine.[1] A piece of work by the same police. So, our young are treated almost in the same way! Only missing, for the moment, are bodies in the river!

In Strasbourg, I met with some workers. "We're no longer certain," they claimed, "what to think about you: the petit bourgeois children of the rich, spoiled, and always wanting more privileges. That, though, is what the communist party and the CGT tell us.[2] I think that, for us, the moment has come to think for ourselves. The images seen on television force us to."

They went on: "If the students in Paris were only 'petit bourgeois, spoiled and egoistical,' why would they try to convince the police, those they call their 'class brothers,' not to repress them, but to join with them, because the goal was to abolish all privileges? And if students were only 'the petit bourgeois quite spoiled by their comfort,' how could they have shown so much courage in the face of repressive acts of violence?"

In the face of reactions—of perplexity or of condemnation of political repression—by a significant part of the public, on the one hand, and of workers on the other, those in authority changed their explanation. They still justified their excessive brutality by the attacks on private property, but they blamed these on "uncontrollable elements" taking part in the movement, notably "the anarchist movement, known for its promotion of violence."

So be it! Assume this is so. Does this justify generalized police repression, without distinctions, including against obviously peaceful demonstrators and even those passing by who had the misfortune of coming into the field of action?

Our indignation equaled our astonishment. We understood that the ruling system contained institutions ready to use violence to defend themselves, but we thought it impossible to see them carry this out against obviously peaceful citizens.

1. In the October 17, 1961, massacre, French police, authorized at the highest level, viciously beat up large numbers of peaceful Algerian demonstrators in the streets of Paris, murdering hundreds and tossing many into the nearby Seine River.
2. The CGT, the General Confederation of Labor, was the largest central trade union organization in France during the first several decades after World War II. Its key leadership positions were held by French communists.

And we were deeply saddened. We saw that the children of workers had been trained and dressed in uniform to repress a movement that wanted to liberate them from their servile and alienated condition. Slaves against slaves, classic rule by those who dominate, everywhere and always, even in the "parliamentary democracies" of the economically "developed" and culturally "advanced" countries. This is what the movement revealed.

For us, yes, our Paris comrades had reason to proclaim: "CRS equals SS!" A well-formulated slogan, in content as well as in form.[3]

To those who saw this slogan as a stylistic exaggeration, we responded: "No. Didn't Hitler's SS begin in the same way, beating peaceful demonstrators, terrorizing them to persuade them not to return to the streets to demand their legitimate rights? The French state presents itself as 'liberal' and 'democratic,' but in what sense does the Paris police violence possess these two traits and not those of fascism?"

We had to, of course, show our solidarity. Immediately, we agreed to it and organized a protest and support demonstration in Strasbourg. We marched from the Palais Universitaire to Place Kléber. It was a central location that most people, including tourists, passed through. Thus, it represented the best-suited location to provoke a maximum effect for our denunciation of state violence.

We carefully prepared ourselves against both fascist attacks and police repression. We expected to confront the same tactic used in Paris: that is, the presence of provocateurs who would act in a way to justify violent intervention by the "forces of order." The CRS would launch tear gas, then charge, and beat people brutally, without distinction, such were the robots or dogs trained to do such.

Each of us got ready as well as possible. Like the others, I armed myself with an iron bar that I hid in appropriate clothes. Then I topped myself with a motorcycle helmet.

For the first time in my life, I had recourse to these two means. Previously, during the anticolonial protests in Algeria, I had gone with bare hands and head like most of the others. Later, in

---

3. The CRS is a special French national security police force well known for violent repression of political demonstrations.

Strasbourg, I understood that peaceful resistance demanded a different sort of defense. We did not support violence; we just wanted to avoid being its victims by defending ourselves.

For my part, I never hit a policeman with my iron bar. I didn't forget that the police officers were "class friends" acting against me by alienated conditioning. My iron bar served solely to deflect blows against me, nothing else.

Very few of us wanted to confront the police "to avenge our Paris comrades." We tried to dissuade those comrades wishing a clash: "Don't fall into the trap of those who wield power. Their victory requires that the enslaved confront them, to the advantage of those who rule. Under the CRS uniform there's a worker who could find no other way to make a living. And if he chose deliberately to take this job of prison guard, for love of violence and obedience to authority, it's because he was conditioned to be transformed into a repressive machine, at the service of its bosses and to the detriment of his social class. It's precisely this process that we have to fight. Thus, be conscious that the cop or the uniformed CRS is, first of all, a brother of our class, more exploited and alienated than we are. Of course, don't let him smash your skull, but try to sensitize his brain to his deadly role, to make him aware of behavior that matches his true interest."

Then we went to demonstrate, shouting, "CRS equals SS, CRS equals SS!"

Of course, I was scared. I put myself on guard. I kept in mind that I was an Algerian on French territory, otherwise known as a *fellagha* (an Algerian rebel), a *fellouze* (nationalist Algerian fighter), a "*bicot*."[4] The cop or the CRS or the fascist would undoubtedly beat me with more cruelty than he would a Frenchman, being certain that in doing so "those above" would cover him, even in the case of assassination.

Even more, if I found myself facing a *pied noir* CRS, my fate would be quickly sealed: "What? . . . You strangled us in your damned *bled* (country village), you shot us, and now you have the

---

4. In French slang, a negative label for an Algerian equivalent to the racist term "nigger" in English.

nerve to come fuck around here, where we live?!" Thus, during the demonstration I placed myself within a group of comrades while explaining my reason, which they quickly understood. They served as an "inner ring" of security in case of an attack. A moving and beautiful fraternal solidarity!

Some of them tried to persuade me to go home: "Thank you for being with us! But we can take action without you." I preferred to remain. Pure madness or generosity, or both at the same time? I couldn't even pose the question. I thought simply that my duty included accepting risks. I encouraged myself with a phrase read in a work of forgotten title and author: "He who is afraid of dying doesn't deserve to live."

In the course of our route, no incident. Our security guards correctly directed participants and watched to ward off any attack on the part of fascists and any provocation coming from our ranks. It was a success. The demonstration took place in a peaceful and orderly fashion, controlled by us.

But, arriving at approaches to Place Kléber, we were blocked. A CRS detachment barred the route. Nevertheless, the first row of protestors tried to force the barricade to get to the square . . . Impossible. The row of CRS firmly prevented any forward movement.

A new attempt . . . in vain. The forward ranks of protestors (I was not among them, by precaution) tried to overcome the police resistance. It was a collision! But while protestors used only their bodies (a resistance technique of nonviolent action, according to Gandhian practice), they first met tear gas, then a charge by police armed with rubber clubs, beating without restraint or pity anyone in their path. Like in Paris.

A wet handkerchief protected me from breathing the tear gas. Also, from the time of the first CRS attack, I managed to flee in time down one of the small streets surrounding the square. Other comrades followed me. Some coughed from inhaling the tear gas, while some had blood on their faces.

To understand the whole reality, two facts should be noted. A quite small minority of our comrades prepared for the demonstration not only with helmets to protect their heads but also gas masks, iron bars, and Molotov cocktails. As I mentioned before, they wanted to confront the "SS" to get revenge for the victims in Paris. But these companions had no need to employ their tools. They were surprised by the unexpected police attack. We only wanted to reach the square peacefully so we could inform the population and passing tourists about the Paris repression. Nothing more.

This act of peaceful citizen protest was denied us. By violence. It was unjustified because there were no store windows broken or vehicles burned by us, nor by others if my memory is correct, and no physical attack on our part against the police.

In Strasbourg after Paris, once again the true faces of "liberalism," of capitalism, of "parliamentarianism," of "democracy" so praised, and of Gaullism revealed themselves.[5]

There were some wounded, a few seriously. Blood ran once again. The beautiful month of May was tainted with yet more red, and the guilty ones were not protestors but representatives of the "democratic" state. Official propaganda called this event Strasbourg's "night of the barricades." That suggested violent actions initiated by rioters. In reality, it was a day of peaceful protest, repressed brutally by the police. Personally, that day I saw no barricades.

After returning from the demonstration, our small group met, with faces anxious, serious. The bloody repression showed us that the movement, in Strasbourg as in Paris, had moved to a higher level: from pacifism and nonviolent resistance, here we were at the stage of violence imposed by state power.

How should we confront it? How would the majority of students, workers, and the population react? For we were a minority in the march toward Place Kléber, around one or two hundred participants.

The student assembly confirmed our concern. The majority were intimidated by the police violence, by the blood of victims. Appeals to respond to the violence by violence failed to receive general approval.

5. Gaullism is the political thought and practice of the state president Charles de Gaulle and his followers.

Some refused that approach by principle. Others denounced it as a way of "falling into the trap" set by the authorities, knowing that in case of violence it would be easy for them (1) to scare the population by evoking the "actions of violent elements who want to bring fire and blood to our country," (2) to thus obtain the support of peaceful citizens, and (3) to justify among them fully unleashing repression against the movement.

There were no further protests like the one that went to Place Kléber.

14

Of the "Spectacle"

Generally, we organized few street protests in Strasbourg compared to Paris. In any case, my group did not participate in the several that took place afterward. We thought them useless if not counterproductive. In effect, who did it serve to smash store windows and burn citizens' cars? Could one admit, without laughing, that they represent the society of "spectacular capitalism" that we needed to destroy?

Yes, certainly! We were opposed to domination by consumption to the detriment of genuine life. We observed how much the former literally destroys the latter. We wanted to exist for our being and not for possessions, as determined by the merchants of unusable gadgets. They mocked us in the show windows. And the car prevented us from using a healthy bicycle.

In our eyes, all superfluous merchandise suffocated our existence, aimed at enslaving it. Exploited as a labor force, then exploited as a consumption force. A vicious closed circle. "Oh you who enter the society of consumption, abandon any hope of one day having an authentic life! Merchandise among the merchandised, that is your fate! To the benefit of the blood-sucking capitalist stockholders."

No, with all our energy, no!

However, openly violent demonstrations by a minority provoked people's anxiety and indignation, legitimate in our opinion. Who, then, actually gained from them? . . . Certainly not the movement. We suspected that this sort of action hid the true actors: not anarchists but police provocateurs.

Of course, the partisans of these violent protests labeled us "dogmatics," if not cowards. For us, this internal division of the movement did it a grave disservice. And we were powerless to resolve the problem.

Influenced by the Situationists, some threw in our face, with a clear sense of self-righteousness, the need to destroy "the Society of the Spectacle" (the title of the 1967 essay by Guy Debord) in which merchandise, "all" merchandise, was "spectacle." This included store windows and their contents, vehicles—in short, everything.

For us, this focus first on the theory of "merchandise spectacle," of the "commercialized spectacular," left us with a vague ambiguous impression and was lacking adequate clarity, if not to say gibberish.

Certainly, Situationists spoke of social classes, of class struggles, of exploitation, of domination. But this dogmatic and repetitive insistence on the "spectacle," employed on each line, in each phrase, concerning everything and nothing and with emphasis, seemed to us to depict something dubious.

In what way is breaking the "spectacle" of a shop window, the "spectacle" of a vehicle (a simple Citröen 2CV, not even a Mercedes or a Cadillac) or even the "spectacle" of a bank office a genuinely confrontational action capable of moving forward the social movement for collective liberation?

Wasn't it too easy an action? . . . And, moreover, a totally ineffective one that gave a negative image to the population. Shouldn't one, to the contrary, attack the "spectacle" (because you adore the term) of citizen alienation in order to make them aware of where to find their real interests?

The enemy, we repeatedly said, was not merchandise, was not the "spectacle," but the alienation of citizens. This is what created victims of merchandise and the "spectacle."

But, to the "talibans" who believed in the theory of the one viewed as a modern Prophet, Debord, as the best of the best, our discourse was totally rejected, labeled retrograde, imbecilic, ignorant, ideological, and so on in the face of their *surah* of "merchandise as spectacle." In brief, they accused us of contesting what we "couldn't understand."

This sort of difficulty reminded us of how much we needed education, how vital it was for the success of every action. We had to find necessary and convincing responses against this framework that saw everything, even time, under the "spectacular" form.[1]

For my part, I confided to my comrades that this theory of the "spectacle" reminded me of the windmills Don Quixote believed were monsters to fight against. I went so far as to say, in substance: "Leave to the intellectuals of well-raised families their fancies about the universal 'spectacle.' In reality, this theory diverts the movement from its real goal: the abolition of the capitalist system and its replacement by a society of freedom and solidarity."

From then on, we spent much time in personal studies, complemented by collective discussions in small groups.

Thus, street demonstrations were strictly limited to those potentially useful for the movement's progress. And we denounced acts of violence claimed by those who said they were members of the movement as wanton, ineffective, and contrary to the goals of our general activity. We condemned them as acts by provocateurs, trying to discredit our movement. The majority of students and workers sided with our opinion.

However, another event took place.

---

1. See chapter 6, "Spectacular Time," in Guy Debord, *The Society of the Spectacle* (orig., 1967; several English translations).

15

Abolition of Borders

On May 21, we learned that Daniel Cohn-Bendit was forbidden to remain in France.[1] In Paris, protest demonstrations proclaimed, "We are all German Jews!"

It was now our turn to act.

We organized our solidarity action. Not solely concerning the person named, but for the principle. In the general assembly, we provided the needed explanations. For us, there were no foreigners in any country because borders were the product of the division of peoples by the social classes that ruled them. Besides, we had read in books about a part of French history: the Revolution of 1789, as well as the Paris Commune of 1871, had foreigners among their members; they were considered as full citizens.

Having myself the foreigner status, I was especially sensitive to the deportation of Cohn-Bendit. It could equally affect me.

One amusing anecdote on this subject. During our discussions, I had occasion to cry out: "We are all German Jews!" . . . By chance, I exchanged glances with a member of the Zionist group present at the assembly. I couldn't help but smile at him. But his face remained frozen.

We had noticed that Strasbourg was located very few kilometers from the German border, so we decided our tactic. We needed

---

1. Daniel Cohn-Bendit was one of the prominent anarchist figures in the March 22 Movement at the Nanterre campus outside of Paris. He became a spokesperson, known to the press, and thus one of the publicized symbolic leaders in the May 1968 revolt. Though studying in France, he had German citizenship and thus was especially vulnerable to French state retaliation.

to go right up to the border and, if possible, cross over and reach the first German locale, the very small town of Kehl, on the other side. And better yet, Daniel Cohn-Bendit, being then in Germany, would come back with us to France.

With a flag of red or black at the front, we marched, protected of course by our security guard formed, as always, by the most burly among us. No incidents.

We arrived at the bridge over the Rhine, linking Strasbourg with Kehl. We chanted, "We are all German Jews!" We passed by the plaque with the name of Strasbourg, marked in red, and another plaque underneath indicating the Rhine. We committed ourselves to go across the bridge toward Kehl. This large and long bridge was built after World War II as a sign of reconciliation. Thus, our demonstration at this location was highly symbolic.

One can imagine my state of mind: an Algerian immigrant in France, marching to cross the border, without a visa, while claiming to be "Jewish" and "German" in company with French comrades as well as others with black skin! . . . My thoughts went to a tragic earlier period: those locked in cattle cars, destined for "obligatory work" or crematorium ovens. We ourselves were going to bring a citizens' "revolution" to the citizens, the miracle of the movement of May–June 1968.

Here my memories weaken. If I'm not mistaken, I would say this. A very welcome surprise greeted us: no police officer or customs guard at the border post at either the French or German side. We passed through quietly until arriving at Kehl. The population looked at us, divided between curiosity and sympathy. We were totally peaceful and calm. I won't say more, not being certain and not wanting to invent what happened.

16

"Enjoy without Restraint"

This slogan was realized to the letter, by some. I think that young people never made as much love or were ever so coupled sexually as during these two months of May and June 1968. One wanted to enjoy everything, the most possible, and first what was most easily available: the body. Let us add that we were in springtime. Flowering—the law of nature.

For my part, my Maoist tendency obliged me to give all my energy to militant action; I considered love and sex a waste of time, to the detriment of urgent and important social action. However, I didn't condemn companions who gave importance to their erotic life. At bottom, I envied them. Despite my ideology being limited to revolutionary action, my erotic impulses often showed themselves at the sight of attractive female companions. However, I managed to silence my desires, replacing my love of girls with love of working people.

Afterthoughts. Were companions right who criticized my denial of physical enjoyment? Would my ideas and actions have been clearer and more effective if I had satisfied the pleasure of eros equally with that of social action? Certainly, erotic pleasure could detract from or lessen attention for the exploited and dominated, but I think it can, to the contrary, equally strengthen and refine one's concern for the people. It seems to me that it's a question of individual character.

From the magnificent May-June 1968, this is my sole regret: not to have known how to reconcile two equally legitimate loves. Dear Edith, what a pity not to have experienced our love!

For me, as for the majority of others, a special form of enjoyment came from interpersonal relations.

I knew the world solely through my experience as a colonized subject and child of a worker, my theatrical studies, the money gained while working at the student restaurant and, during summer vacation, in a beer factory, the rent I paid for my attic room, my travel from one place to another, and finally my friendships and several previous love affairs.

Here I discovered another world: that of spontaneous and generous exchange of ideas, of egalitarian cooperation in creative actions, of camaraderie based on sharing common ideals of freedom and solidarity. My daily life enriched itself from non-merchandised interactions, not utilitarian in the usual sense of the term.

I was amazed by the ease with which persons, unknown to each other, calmly and with pleasure posed every question imaginable to each other, and responded to these with courtesy. One would have thought we were all familiar with each other.

This phenomenon was very widespread among us students, previously cloistered by "inclination" in our "individuality." The famous separation between people, to the benefit of rulers, was replaced by spontaneous, free, enriching communication in favor of those no longer wanting to be "subjects divided to be enslaved."

Of course, between strangers, the friendly use of the more familiar *tu* (for "you") replaced the ceremonial *vous*. This came about without decree by a state authority, as had occurred during the Revolution of 1789. This shows, then, how much individual freedom implies and encourages freedom for everyone and reciprocal solidarity. I called this *freedom in solidarity*. In effect, I would consider freedom without solidarity to be egoism, if not to say behavior to the detriment of others, and I conceived of solidarity as a constriction unless it came out of free will.

That is why I held myself separate from two visions. The first, that of a certain Stalinist Marxism, was *imposed* solidarity, in reality a fiction because it excluded free choice. In fact, it was about servile obedience to leaders, presented as essential "discipline." The second vision presented itself as anarchist. It conceived of individual freedom as a necessity without relation to, and even incompatible with, solidarity. In other words: "Let each take care of things on his or her own!"

I would respond: "And what of those whose socioeconomic and cultural conditions kept them from knowing how to get by on their own?"

"They need only find the solution! No need for a guide or authority."

"But what of someone who, while respecting their autonomy, provides selfless assistance? Why not?"

"Everyone should work it out on their own."

I explained that I probably would not have become conscious of the need to free myself from my alienation if not for the assistance of generous non-authoritarian persons. Thus, I can't conceive of freedom without solidarity or vice versa.

"Enjoy without restraint!" they threw back at me.

I objected: "On the condition that one doesn't block the enjoyment of others."

"But why do you have to consider others? . . . Enjoy your freedom, and each his or her own. And all will go well!"

To this proposal, I have an amusing but significant anecdote.

One pleasantly sunny afternoon, I found myself with friends at a sidewalk serving as the terrace of a bar frequented by students. It made an angle between two streets, quite close to the Palais Universitaire.

Suddenly, a Congolese friend was coming toward us, quite excited, calling out: "I had her! I had her!"

"What then?"

"A *white* girl!" he responded, triumphantly.

"So what, a *white* girl?"

"I made love to a *white* girl and, at the moment of orgasm, while I was on top of her, I cried, 'Long live Africa!'"

We burst out laughing. Holy Manuel! (That was our friend's name.)

At the same time, we were a little embarrassed. Others had heard his phrase. What did they think of our sexual "conqueror"?

We made him sit down, then tried to calm him.

We knew that Manuel lacked political education and was not at all a militant. For him, the movement signified only vacation and occasions to satisfy his libido, nothing more. He had just succeeded, this time according to his most ambitious wish.

In this adventure, the colonized, dominated, and alienated mentality of Manuel showed itself, certainly in a comic if not ridiculous manner, but it was shown. If not, how to explain this "Long live Africa"?

He thought to free that continent of its miseries by an erotic pleasure conquered from a supposed "representative" of "white" rulers, an achievement by a "representative" of the people with black skin. Ah! What erotico-social liberation!

This event was the object of long examination between us, first at the café and afterward in our group. But our analysis was seriously limited. As good Marxist-Leninist Maoists, we distrusted psychology and psychoanalysis. Thus, in the theoretical domain, we were completely disarmed before the question of eros. We dismissed this theme as "petit bourgeois," a "serious deviation" from "revolutionary duty."

However, more than once, during the night or when waking, my body reminded me of the existence of that eros within. I ignored it quite easily when thinking of the categorical imperative "to make revolution."

17

"Imagination to Power"

Never were my own imagination and those of my companions shown with more inventiveness, brilliance, and richness in every domain.

Even if one didn't participate directly in the movement, one could understand its creativity by taking in the huge number of posters produced and slogans written on the walls. Among the former, I liked especially the two reproduced below. They showed the two matrices of the movement: the first, youth, and the second, the factory worker.[1] Both concerned and spoke to my personal experience.

Labor

I said that I was the child of a shoe factory worker. A hundred wage laborers, many machines, and human beings reduced to being

1. Above, left: "Be young and shut up." Right: "Don't let yourself be exploited."

ancillaries of machines. Thus, the poster on the right reflected a reality I knew well already.

During school vacations, I often brought lunch to my father at the factory. I saw there how the labor force was exploited. I observed its most obvious manifestation: sweat drenching the brow and cheeks of my father. It fell drop by drop onto the machine. And he had no time to dry off. The incessant motion of the machine, on the one hand, and the foreman, on the other, coming and going continuously, ensuring that those riveted to the machine continued their mechanical movements, totally dependent on the moving machine.

I had poignant pity for my father and his companions of misfortune. The hell spoken of by the religious made me smile by comparison with that observed in the manufacture of shoes. The only sin of the workers was in the financial condition of their families; they were incapable of providing for enough education to allow their offspring to escape this earthly damnation. They sold their bodies to a boss in exchange for a wage fixed at the lowest level, limited solely to what was needed to renew labor power. This was and still is called maximization of profit (for the boss and stockholders) to the detriment of the unfortunate human machines.

They suffered the "original sin" of their parents—poverty.

In turn, their children, becoming adults, became victims as well. Poverty led to poverty. My participation in the movement of May-June 1968 aimed at eliminating this infamous social injustice in order to give human beings the same opportunities from the start.

It seemed to me, at that time, that something like that was materializing in China: students and intellectuals were being sent to the factories and among peasants for a certain amount of time. The operation aimed to decrease the distance between the privileged and the deprived in order to create a society where manual labor and intellectual labor would be equally divided between members of the community—the consequence being just access to social wealth for all.

This is why some of us believed fundamentally in "going to the people" and in sharing their life conditions for a certain period.

Workers would learn from us, and we would learn from them. This initiative was a first step toward the abolition of the privileges we, the students, possessed. We were convinced, against the advice of other students, that to fulfill a certain fixed period of time in manual labor did not imply a loss of time in our intellectual education. To the contrary, it reinforced it by providing a practical social complement. In this way, I experienced my placement as a beer factory worker in Strasbourg. From this I left with more appropriate ideas, stronger and more firmly held.

Youth

As to the poster on the above left, ah!, how much I suffered from paternalism, that primary form of authoritarianism. With bad or "good" intentions, it aimed to stifle in me every free and creative energy, reducing me to a sheep in a herd, to a screw in a mechanism, to a submissive subject, to one dominated and exploited.

The Qur'anic school preacher of my youngest childhood, the schoolmaster in primary school, the lycée teacher, older persons, too many of them, wanted to transform me into a "good student," a "good citizen"—in other words, a subject obeying a ruler.

Even my dear father showed this preoccupation. He regretted that I completed primary school and wished that I should become a worker like himself as soon as possible in order to better the economic situation of my family. I owe solely to my mother the concern that I go on with school so as, she affirmed, "to escape poverty and not live the cruel life of your father."

Then I saw the above poster on the condition of youth. The artist shows it in the most complete, significant, and striking manner. The one who puts his dark and ugly hand over the mouth of the youth, with whom I immediately identified, was General de Gaulle, the president of France. His tall, shadowy, immense stature symbolized here the archetype of all that is a castrating authority.

Anonymity

Consider now the two posters. Their authors were not looking for media recognition or financial gain. The anonymous signature at the bottom verifies this: "People's Workshop / Ex-School of Fine Arts."

At Strasbourg, we also produced the same type of posters, signed "Graphics Workshop of the Autonomous University of Strasbourg." Above is an example.[2]

We appreciated the anonymity. It reflected recognition and praise for the collective dimension of creativity, where art shows itself spontaneously through unidentified citizens, thus reflecting a communitarian vision.

Add to this the works' liberating dimension. Could their authors have achieved them within a "school of fine arts" under the control of a "teaching" elite? Didn't they need the existence of a "people's workshop," autonomous and free from all limiting control?

Let us also note the anonymous signatures of articles in militant newspapers and tracts. One found there solely the name of the organization, not the author or authors. This was the same with the famous Situationist pamphlet of 1967.

I appreciated this erasure of the individual in favor of the collectivity. I saw in this a positive reaction against the excessive cult of

2. "Here are some of us loving the pleasure of loving without reserve, passionately enough to offer to love the sumptuous bed of a revolution."

the individual, a demonstration of modesty, respect for others, and collective fusion.

Of course, I generally knew who wrote what. But the anonymous presentation pleased me. I thought more of the author.

18

The State Backed into a Corner and "Hyenas" on the Watch

On May 24, we admired on television the impressive Paris demonstration called by the central CGT trade union. Throughout the country were other demonstrations.

We were jubilant. If the most important workers' union embraced the movement, we had an avenue for hope!

We saw proof of this in the immediate reaction of the enemy: fear. The president, General de Gaulle, cast his bait on television: he announced the organization of a June referendum on participatory decision-making for workers in enterprises and for students in the universities.

We assembled our group in one of the university rooms. We feared seeing students fall into the trap set by the one called "the great smart-ass," de Gaulle. But not much effort was needed to avoid potential demobilization. We learned that the response to the chief of state's proposal was another demonstration in Paris, with new barricades, and . . . *nec plus ultra*, the burning of the Bourse![1]

For this, we were quite proud but also very anxious. We knew that the Bourse was the very symbol of the capitalist system, its heart or, if you like, its brain. The fire thus took on great significance. We struggled to discover the real authors of this event: comrades or provocateurs.

We contacted friends in Paris, but we couldn't find irrefutable proof. However, basically we were pleased.

1. The Paris stock exchange.

Another trap of the great smart-ass. On May 25, at the Ministry of Labor in Paris, negotiations began between the trinity of trade unions, employers, and the government.

It was our first quite serious concern. We tried to understand what this signified. Would employers and the government be able to buy off the trade union bureaucratic elite?

We were scared, very scared. What we knew of the matter was this: one never saw bureaucrats renounce their privileges in favor of a revolution eliminating all privilege, including their own.

On May 27, we learned the epilogue. The content of the so-called Grenelle agreement: increased unemployment benefits and base wages, the workday gradually reduced to forty hours a week, the age of retirement lowered, revised collective agreements, recognition of trade union sections in enterprises, and increased trade union rights.

To the horde of hungry dogs, the owners threw some bones to chew on. Some affordable employer concessions to suffocate social change aiming to eliminate ownership itself.

This was our conclusion in the group, which was then presented and discussed at the general assembly. General dismay.

On May 27, we also learned of the meeting held in Paris at the Charléty stadium, in the presence of Pierre Mendès-France.[2] The following day, there was François Mitterand, who, reckoning a vacant regime, announced his candidacy for the presidency with the slogan "people's government without exclusiveness and without outdated political bias."[3]

"What?" we said to ourselves. "Once again the 'socialist' hyenas to the rescue of capitalism by recuperating revolutionary action?"

The people's government that we wanted should be that of the workers, the citizens, not that of the party bureaucrats, whose collusions with the capitalist bourgeoisie were well-known.

2. Pierre Mendès-France was French prime minister in the mid-1950s and leader of a small moderate socialist party. He was popular among some on the left for having negotiated French withdrawal from Indochina and Tunisia.

3. François Mitterand was a prominent mainstream democratic socialist party politician who ran as the left-center opposition candidate for president against de Gaulle in 1965.

We had studied various social democratic attempts to suffocate authentic proletarian revolutions in Russia, Germany, France, Italy, and Spain—everywhere.

For us, our movement's objective was to establish a genuine workers' regime (workers-peasants-employees) allied with intellectuals and in the form of self-management. Our model was that of the Russian soviets.[4]

On this subject, within the group were very lively discussions. They opposed partisans of "proletarian dictatorship" to those, including myself, having a contrary point of view. In the name of what seemed the libertarian Maoism of the Cultural Revolution, we feared the formation of a new form of bureaucratic elite practicing a new form of exploitation of the people.

We definitely wanted a society where every form of exploitation and domination would be banned, whatever the label. Consequently, we refused two alternatives. On the one hand, we rejected a private capitalism, softened by crumbs to the people; this was our interpretation of the appearance of Mendès-France and Mitterand. On the other hand, we did not want a nomenklatura that, on the pretext of a "dictatorship of the proletariat," would take over the state to gain privileges, as in the USSR.

My comrades and I that evening stayed together late into the night. It was impossible to sleep. We thought the moment was quite serious. What would leaders of the movements do? For our part, what would we do?

The next day, we learned that the secretary-general of the CGT, Georges Séguy himself, went to Renault factories in Boulogne-Billancourt. He presented the agreements to the strikers.

Against his expectation, they voted to pursue the strike.

"Ah!" . . . Our relief was immense. Our group, then the general assembly, expressed our joy. Hope continued to shine. Our strongest wish was that workers would finally see the nature of their trade union "management": the common link between the material privileges they enjoyed and the owners' interests.

---

4. I repeat, one more time, that at the time we did not know that the soviets were later taken over and then reined in, authoritatively, by the Bolshevik party.

19
Apotheosis: The Turning Point

On May 29 we heard the most thrilling news. The "hero" of the anti-Nazi resistance, "*the* President," "*the general*," de Gaulle abandoned l'Elysée and took refuge, like a czar, like any common dictator of the "Third World," in an army base.[1]

We eventually learned that he went to the German city of Baden-Baden, the seat of the commander in chief of French forces in that country. When I learned the name of the henchman in chief, I was pleasantly surprised.

"Ah! Again General Massu! . . . The hangman of the Battle of Algiers![2] . . . Truly, for colonized Algerian people or dominated French people, the caste of those who massacred is the same. . . . Once again, history repeats itself."

I was reminded of another sinister author of massacre, Louis Eugène Cavaignac. He distinguished himself by his criminal "smoke killings" of Algerians, then, upon returning to France, repressed the June 1848 grassroots revolution in Paris.[3]

To return to de Gaulle, I discovered then his real nature: bourgeois, defender of the bourgeoisie, full of phrases to impress an

---

1. L'Elysée: The French presidential residence.

2. General Massu led an elite division of parachutists in 1956–1957 to suppress the FLN nationalist movement in Algiers through mass arrests and extensive use of torture.

3. As an increasingly prominent military officer in the ongoing French war to establish a colony in Algeria in the 1830s and 1840s, Louis Eugène Cavaignac was infamous as the first to authorize the massacre tactic of smoke asphyxiation, which he used in 1844 against a large number of Algerian refugees hiding in a cave. Several years later, as the appointed French general/dictator, he bloodily suppressed the massive Paris grassroots revolt.

idiot. The more I saw the "Great One" present himself on the television screen—an obligatory manipulated production—the more I perceived the contemptible side of his character: bourgeois in body and soul, in the most miserly sense of the term. A modern Adolph Thiers,[4] nothing more if not for his tall height and prominent nose. "Certainly," I thought, "without hesitating he would give the order to fire on the people of Paris if he thought it necessary. If not, why did he meet with the butcher guard dog Massu? . . . Wasn't it really the chief of state's *threat* against our movement?"

Some among us asked what the two lascars said to each other. "What difference does it make?" I responded. "We don't need to know. Isn't the act in itself eloquent enough? . . . In other words: 'You shits![5] If you persist, I'll send Massu and his henchmen, and he'll do to you what he did in Algiers.'"

Additionally, we knew the reality of one fact. For the first time in the history of France, around *ten million* strikers occupied their factories, generally with a red flag as their emblem. We were in the presence of the most important general strike of the twentieth century! It lasted for many days and weeks across the nation. It was decided by workers themselves, against the advice of their bureaucratic trade union "managers" and against the so-called institutions of the "left." These prison guards of the proletariat showed themselves unable to manipulate the workers' revolt. Clearly, it was political, not economic: not for secondary improvements, but a change of status. Down with bosses! Down with capitalism! Long live worker power in the factories! Long live self-management!

This was how we read this extraordinary and powerful social movement. To paraphrase Mao, we understood that "the spark had started a prairie fire."

We were thus in the midst of a decisive reversal in favor of a people's movement.

Another sign of fundamental social rupture: in the wake of strikes, most factories shut down. The economy of the country was

---

4. Adolph Thiers was the French political leader who authorized the tragic large-scale military suppression of the revolutionary 1871 Paris Commune.

5. We learned that this word had been pronounced by de Gaulle during an interministerial meeting on May 19, using the phrase: "Reforms, yes; the shits, no."

paralyzed. Thus, decreasing the surplus value of the stockholders and creating serious problems of daily life for citizens. This couldn't continue for long.

In addition, part of the intelligentsia was in solidarity with the movement. The symbol of this was Jean-Paul Sartre. He took on the editorial direction of the Maoist newspaper, *The Cause of the People*, to let it escape problems from the state. He himself even distributed copies in the street and ended up in prison. However, he was rapidly liberated. The leader of existentialism even went to the proletarian "reservation" of Boulogne-Billancourt. Hoisted onto a container, he expressed his support.

In the face of all of these extraordinary events, our heads were spinning, made dizzy by coming to the point of no return: the reversal of the ruling social system and its replacement by something better.

All of this was coming about without elections, without "palace" maneuvers, without an armed coup d'état, without a Day of August 10, 1792, against the Tuileries,[6] without an attack on the Winter Palace,[7] without a Bolshevik "avant-garde Party," and without a long Maoist grassroots war.

This is how the slogan "Be realistic, demand the impossible!" which could appear as a simple play of words, a utopian desire from a juvenile mind provoking at best a paternalist smile or at worst a scornful laugh, became reality. This assumption followed the flight of the chief of state—and not just anyone, but the author of the grandiloquent word, "Greatness"!

We were happy to find ourselves at this stage.

But we were also anxious. Our group came together almost on a permanent basis. Quite urgently, we had to examine decisive questions: How would the army react? And those of the rest of Europe? And that of the world imperialist policeman, the United States? . . . Aren't they all protectors of the dominant capitalist system?

From this time on, how could we resist? How could we win?

6. The French Revolution's decisive insurrectionist attack on the royal palace that led to the monarchy's formal abolition just six weeks later.
7. The Bolshevik-led attack on the Winter Palace in Petrograd on October 25, 1917, as a final step in deposing the Provisional Government in Russia.

Are we now on the verge of civil war? . . . We thought about the most recent one, the Spanish: the armed uprising of the fascist general Franco met by the republican resistance.[8] In a parallel case, will we act more effectively?

We had no appropriate military training, no underground party of the Bolshevik type, no precise political line, no centralized organization. We didn't know the attitude of party leaders or of the trade union comprising the most workers: the "communist" party and the CGT.

According to the given formula, the hour was very grave, decisive. The first phase of what we wanted with all our energy to happen had arrived: abdication of the ruling regime.

But it surprised us, as proven by our lack of preparation to confront the situation positively.

Our sole hope relied on a hypothesis: that part of the army, mobilized against us by the legal president of the nation to "repress illegal subversion," would start coming to our side, at best, or would not obey orders, at worst.

In this period of extreme tension, of utmost risk, of total indecision, I thought of my life, still short, of a possible armed repression, of the need to confront it, of eventually learning how to bear arms, to kill "brothers" clothed in military uniforms, to be killed. What a horror! What sadness for me, who fought only for goodness and beauty!

I knew that for some time certain comrades, a minority, went regularly into the woods surrounding Strasbourg where they trained at handling arms. I was never invited to join in, and I did not dream of proposing it.

Being born in a violent colonial society, I hated violence. All while being persuaded that "power comes from the barrel of a gun" (Mao). Yes, my behavior was contradictory. I suffered from it deeply without being able to talk about it. All of my comrades were aware of the role of violence as the "midwife of history." And I was too.

However, I was glad to remind myself of the comrades' military training. Perhaps circumstances would oblige me to that which

8. In 1936.

I loathed: to rejoin them and receive their learning. That meant having recourse to arms, to the eventual flowing of blood, despite my revulsion.

I strongly aspired to social change, but peacefully. However, I knew that change was always the product of violence, with rare exceptions, such as the Gandhian anticolonial action in India and that of Martin Luther King for civil rights in the United States.

However, if circumstances demanded it, I prepared myself for the horrible, but only as armed self-defense against a first attack with arms. Hoping not to see our resistance suffer the fate of the antifascist Spanish, I saw the troubling door open to the unknown, obliging us to pass through and to resolve ourselves to "achieve the impossible," the victory of our movement, of social justice, but through the most detestable means, by arms.

I had few illusions. I remembered the successive epilogues in Paris of the June 1848 days, then of the 1871 Commune. I did not forget the menace brandished by de Gaulle: General Massu! . . . If I needed to die, it remained for me to cry out, as did the earlier Paris insurgents: "Long live the universal social republic!" . . . However, at my core, I wished to live; it wasn't funny to die so young. And what's more, it was more useful to continue living, to pursue the struggle in one way or another.

A cul-de-sac! . . . I had the horrible and desperate sense that that's where we were.

20

The Ebb Tide Begins with the Treason of the "Watch Dogs"

"God! Save me from my friends! As to my enemies, I'll deal with them." Watch out for the Judas of the situation.

Alas! Alas! Alas! . . . Those who pretended "genuinely" to represent working people and who wanted change in their favor, the leaders of the "communist" party and the CGT trade union, took fright at the liberation struggle of the same working people.

How could this be explained unless by the fear of losing their *privileges* as bureaucratic leaders? They knew that this would be the case if civil war broke out to construct a system of social justice and solidarity. They were aware that the wielders of state power, at risk themselves of being thrown out, would not hesitate to launch armed conflict if it seemed the last recourse. They had the military force on their side: General Massu! Those rules imposed themselves, in dictatorships as in "liberal" regimes. The army is not solely an institution of defense against foreign attacks, it also serves against internal "subversion," even from the people. To accuse the latter of "playing the game of the foreign enemy" is a propagandistic argument.

"We must know how to end a strike!" declared trade union leaders, subordinate to the bosses, while evoking a sense of "responsibility," of "reality," of "workers' higher interests."

May 25 and 26, the elite of "communist" party bureaucrats and their transmission belt, the trade union with the most workers, obtained the Grenelle agreements. I spoke of them earlier.

It sealed the complicity between employers and "shepherds" of the workers. Thus, the infamous trinity prevailed: exploiting capitalist stockholders (conserving their surplus value), ruling state leaders (keeping their advantages), and "communist" bureaucracy as well as political auxiliary "trade union" (maintaining their privileges). It was the sacred union against those who kept the factories functioning by their muscles and sweat.

And this in the name of "democracy," that of the craftiest, richest, and most powerful against the most honest, poorest, and weakest.

The organs of ruling propaganda, so-called information, presented this ignoble pact as "realism," with a "sense of responsibilities," and treated those who contested it as "leftists," a "peril to the nation," "complicit with the Eastern bloc," and the like.

And the strikes concluded, in exchange for minimal and temporary corporate concessions.

The consequence: a return to the usual subway-job-sleep daily grind. The resigned bitterness was justified, eased only by bones thrown to a pack of starving, enraged dogs. Concessions to the "riffraff" saved what was essential: capitalism adapted itself to the crisis. Once again in the history of popular uprisings, not only those in France, what prevented army intervention was the complicity of "socialists" and "communists," who assumed the role of firefighters.

Another harmful consequence: on May 30, we were sad to see the demonstration in support of the existing regime. Encouraged by the betrayals against a just social change, a parade of the well-off in their fine clothes marched in Paris, on the Champs-Elysées. About three hundred thousand people, according to the prefecture of police; a million claimed by the Gaullists.

In the first row among them marched the ex-combatant for the Spanish republic and against the fascist regime of General Franco, the writer André Malraux. What degradation!

What could be done when the regime's nomenklatura and the caste of fake representatives of the workers allied themselves to block the popular movement? And, on the other side, a lack of organization capable of rejecting this compromise?

On May 31, the press brought us very grave news: tanks were headed in the direction of Paris, while at the ORTF,[1] the police

---

1. The ORTF was the national agency for government-run public radio and TV.

and the army were putting an end to the occupation. We considered the loss of this central information source to be a fatal blow to the movement. We no longer possessed the country's most powerful communication voice.

And tanks toward Paris? . . . How could our comrades oppose them? . . . Had they predicted this action of the regime?

In my group and despite our readings of Mao Zedong's writing on this theme, we had spoken of the military aspect quite vaguely, so vaguely that it seemed this eventuality was foreseen only verbally, in a dogmatic way, without truly believing it. In the militant press, I had the same impression.

Generally, during the whole period of May and June, it seemed to me that the military side was never seriously considered. I explained it to myself by the basic orientation of the movement—peaceful action—and by the illusion that in Western Europe, in a "democratic" country even, the military question was not to be expected. How many times, in raising this problem, had I heard comrades reply, while smiling or breaking out laughing: "Ha, Ha! We're not in the Eastern bloc. Nor in the Third World!"

"Perhaps!" I had finally thought. And now here was the reality of tanks converging on Paris, confirming my fear. "Yeah, yeah!" I said at the time "Bourgeois democracy exists as long as it suits the elite. If it's threatened, the sword is raised; in other words, the tanks would appear. First, General Massu, and now the tanks!"

More than once, I was preoccupied with the military aspect, and I spoke about it to my comrades. But I only met obvious skepticism.

"You come from the Third World, comrade! That's why you're obsessed with the army. Here in France, it's different. The army would never dare to oppose the will of the people!"

I objected: "And in June 1848? And with the Paris Commune of 1871?"

"All of that was in the past! We're now in the modern period."

What to say in the face of unanimity? . . . "Perhaps they're right," I was forced to conclude.

The time came, nevertheless, when it seemed to me that I was right: "And now, de Gaulle to see General Massu?"

To that, they couldn't respond. I saw only tense faces.

However, we all understood one thing: it was too late; we weren't prepared. And the several comrades who valiantly asserted, "So, we'll move on to armed struggle!" failed to calm us.

The reality showed us the grave naïveté that had led to neglecting the military aspect of the movement. I was extremely pained. "At bottom, past or present, dictatorial Third World or democratic developed countries, the ultimate recourse is always the army! To not take account of this factor is to condemn oneself to failure."

Let us return to the central base of action, the occupied Palais Universitaire. The threat presented itself: to be forcefully evacuated by the police. Possibly fascist groups would try a surprise attack by successfully penetrating inside to start a battle against us that would give the excuse for police intervention.

We thus took necessary precautions: to block all possible exits, including doors and windows, and to set up permanent security groups, taking turns, day and night. This final measure worked at night in a special way, when only students remained behind the walls to assure continuity of the occupation.

Another threat we had to avert was an intentional fire. The fascists would have loved to bring it about somehow, discreetly; afterward, they would accuse us, "They burned up the university, the barbarians!" That would have, first, justified police intervention and, second, provoked the indignation of the population against us.

Thus, taking our turns, every two hours, we slept and then took our rounds, a flashlight in the hand, a helmet on the head, and an iron bar in the other hand.

I contemplated. . . . Violence comes always, without exception, from partisans of domination and exploitation of human beings. Even when people revolt and resort to violence, in fact that is simply *counter*violence, responding primordially to the bloodsuckers of humanity. It's self-defense, and its violent aspect is *imposed* by the enemy. Gandhi and Martin Luther King represented exceptions to the rule.

And, finally, I noted the repetition of history, returning to several years earlier, between 1960 and 1962, when I was fifteen to seventeen years old. At that time, the OAS (Secret Army Organization), the fascist group of *pieds-noirs* opposed to Algerian independence, resorted to every possible massacre of native civilians.

To avoid their attacks, I took part in security and self-defense groups at night. There, inside or on the terraces of buildings, I slept for two hours, then, with two companions, inspected the surroundings for two hours.

Thus, to fight against fascism in Algeria, then to fight in Strasbourg against social fascism in France, it was all the same, parallel.

I don't recall if there was some fascist attempt to penetrate the university interior. In any case, we were ready to maintain our control without violence.

Sometimes, instead of sleeping, we took advantage of the calm of night to pursue our excellent, invaluable discussions on how to resist and to continue the movement.

We observed the beginning of the retreat. We had to know how to confront it. Various options presented themselves.

Some looked to pursue the struggle through peaceful means, among students and workers. The technique would involve increasing the sites of free self-management in solidarity, throughout the territory and in every social domain.

Others, to the contrary, were persuaded that the regime, for the moment on guard, would prevent that action by any means, legal or illegal. Thus, the struggle had to be pursued underground and by armed resistance. From then on, the question arose: Would students and especially workers agree to this? "Revolutionaries are like fish in the water," affirmed Mao Zedong. In France, how many citizens would accept the role of water?

I noticed the striking contrast between the calm freshness of the night and the feverishly harsh nature of our discussions. Who knows why, but I thought of Shakespeare, of the poetically starry night under which assassins sent by the tyrant stabbed their innocent victims. We were the future victims; the assassins would be the fascists, the CRS, or soldiers sent by the "legitimate" head of state.

Never in my life had I such scorn for the state and those who controlled it. Legal criminals to whom citizen alienation, as consenting slaves, had democratically confided their destiny.

Yet one more time, we evoked the 1871 Paris Commune, the massacres ordered by Thiers and committed by generals. Thousands of workers and ordinary citizens assassinated for wishing simply to self-manage their own existence without being exploited or dominated by a minority class of social parasites.

Seated in a circle, drinking coffee to keep us awake, exchanging glances of warm camaraderie, we knew we had neither the experience nor training required by this delicate moment we lived in and especially by the future we had to confront. We were conscious of being neither tacticians nor strategists of revolution. And we had the bitter conviction that we had no leaders up to the situation. We felt like lost militants.

Nevertheless, we forced ourselves to resort to all our intelligence, to all our knowledge, to all of our young experience to plan our future action. We were neither followers nor leaders, simply companions putting their "imagination to power" to keep from accepting the ebb tide and to discover how to continue riding the beautiful flow tide we had created.

Never more than in that precise moment of my life have I observed and understood how much radical social change needs preparation, education, and theoretical and practical knowledge, all while knowing there were no readymade formulas to apply. Social life could not be reduced to mathematical equations. It came back to me how the more I played chess or the game of go, the more complicated it became and how much time was needed to master multiple and diverse actions for oneself and to predict the actions of the adversary. I recalled reading *The Art of War* by Sun Tzu. I took time to reread that short essay. I noticed there that our defeat was predicted at about the fifth century BC: "Don't let your enemies unite."

They were united: employers, government, parties, and trade unions of the "left."

"He who knows his enemy as he knows himself will in a hundred battles never be defeated. He who knows himself but does not know the enemy will be victorious one time out of two. He who knows neither his enemy nor himself is always in danger."

We were victorious in launching the movement, but we knew neither ourselves nor the enemy sufficiently.

In effect, as to the two bodies of the ruling class's ultimate defense, the police and army, we didn't know how to arouse their benevolent neutrality toward radical social change, much less how to rally them to our side. We already had too much to accomplish with university students, lycée students, workers, and a part of the broader population. We had neither time nor persons to deal with police officers and drafted soldiers as well. We knew that what was impossible in Strasbourg was also impossible in Paris. However, history books taught us that without these two elements, the police and army, insurrection never brought positive results. To the contrary, it led to painful defeat.

To return to the game of go, our situation seemed obvious. We were encircled by an assembly of united forces.

I was only twenty-two and a half years old, and my companions more or less the same age. Too young to know how to face the most difficult possible undertaking: a genuine victorious workers' revolution. Our own movement also surprised us in its lack of preparation to take on this task up to its final goal.

However, we had no regrets for what we had been able to gain. It was already something. We had achieved the impossible: ten million workers on strike! Thousands if not millions of future "managers" of the system contested it by occupying universities and lycées, and even by raising barricades; the head of state in flight, obliged to call on the army, then make an agreement with the mercenaries of the "communist" party and the CGT. Not bad, no, even so?

However, a phrase resonated in our brains. We told ourselves: "Those who make revolution halfway only dig their own graves" (Saint-Just).[2] No! We did not want the grave, unless the struggle demanded it; rather, we wanted to continue the fight—but, alas, without knowing how.

Those nights it was impossible to sleep, despite our extreme fatigue. Nor could we cry in the corner for relief, so heavily weighed our failure. I've said that we had no confidence in the "leaders," all the more since they didn't know how to avoid certain retreat. We

2. Louis Antoine de Saint-Just was a powerful military advisor and political figure, a close ally of Robespierre, on the Committee of Public Safety during the French Revolution.

had only ourselves to find solutions for our most urgent protection, to know how to withdraw in good order, with a minimum of damage and trauma. June 12, I was painfully bitter: the regime, now strong again, decreed that several extreme-left organizations be dissolved. Among these was the UJC(ML), the organization I sympathized with. "Encircled" and "absorbed."

One question, however, tapped my mind. Why wasn't the Situationist International itself also targeted by the decree? Its members and ideas seemed to me to have played an important subversive role. Furthermore, I had no doubt about the intelligence of the state power wielders to determine, fight against, and eliminate those they considered their real enemies.

I conveyed my concern to some of the comrades. They had no response. The enigma remained very much on our minds.

For us, students in Strasbourg, the retreat presented itself on the same June 12. The police intervened to force us to evacuate "our" Palais Universitaire. We knew the futility of any resistance but also understood the need to evade arrest, knowing the negative consequences that would follow. We avoided encirclement by dispersing.

We thus abandoned our dear "red and black base of freedom." Oh! How much we loved it, how much we had there lived exhilarating hours of freedom and solidarity, how much this place had become, through our self-management, a genuine place of knowledge and authentic existence, preparing us for the most beautiful of professions: to live with dignity.

While leaving, several among us, including me, began openly to cry. My stomach tightened. From now on, I had to face an unknown destiny. We had no "rear bases" in either town or country, thus no Long March to undertake to rejoin them.[3] Only a long wandering life remained.

One final event saddened me deeply while also leaving me quite perplexed. On June 30, during the second round of legislative

---

3. The "Long March" of the Chinese Communist army was a retreat of over four thousand miles through the countryside in 1934 and 1935 to allow its successful escape from Kuomintang encirclement and repression and its revival in a safe rural base.

elections, the majority went to . . . the Gaullists. I couldn't understand this. How to explain such a result?

Discussions with comrades of my group provided no convincing clarification. Nor did the militant press. Nor did the Situationists. Nor did "leaders" of the various tendencies of the movement.

In particular, I had read quite carefully and discussed with my comrades the May 30 tract of the central committee of the Marxist-Leninist Communist Party of France. Entitled, in all caps, "Against the monopolies, against fascism, organize revolutionary peoples' power," it concluded with this call to action, again all capitalized: "Unity at the base and in action! Organize everywhere revolutionary action committees! Anti-monopolist and anti-fascist united front! Long live revolutionary people's power."[4]

But *how* could we organize these "action committees"? I didn't know how, nor did my comrades in the group. And we waited for more indications, but in vain.

Once again, I noted with sorrow my shortcomings in political-social matters. "What a mediocre citizen I am! . . . Too ignorant!"

I also thought, with bitterness: "The leaders in Paris as well." Observing the result, I noted that they had launched a movement without sufficiently reflecting, without predicting all the consequences, especially the head of state's recourse to the army and also to legislative elections where the regime would emerge victorious.

I had wanted this especially from the leaders who proclaimed themselves, and perhaps were, the best informed, the most brilliant: the Situationists. But, just as much, I wanted this from the Marxist-Leninist Maoist leaders, as well as the Trotskyists. Their prestigious references and their ambition to lead had not given them the ability to carry out the needed social reversal.

Thus, I was too disillusioned to recognize that these leaders, at least, had the merit of having put all their energy into achieving the revolutionary ideal. I was too disappointed to admit that, despite everything, these leaders had known how to discover the weakest aspects of the capitalist system and to attack them in a way

---

4. Capitalized in the original. "Tract du 30 mai 1968," http://lesmaterialistes .com/tract-30-mai-1968.

that provoked in France a historic social movement of extraordinary size.

My final observation was the most bitter. The movement in which I participated heart and soul, with millions of others— university students, teachers, lycée students, and manual workers, men and women—this movement had not been anticipated, properly prepared, or well organized, in a way to give the expected results.

Its size was a surprise for all of us. And its failure was very rapid once the moment came for the decisive toppling of the regime. Check and mate by his "Greatness," the general, because he had the sense for organization and maneuver. To the contrary, our go strategy failed because of its spontaneity. One doesn't improvise tactics and social strategy from one day to the next, or because one believes oneself to be a strategist. It's still necessary to bring to the task genuine abilities, demonstrated in practice.

Despite my inadequate politico-social education, this very painful conclusion was clear to me.

I remembered especially one significant fact. I was familiar enough with factory workers to convince me of one reality.

Certainly, at first glance, at first contact, it seemed that the first and principal concern of workers was "economic," as Lenin stated: higher wages and better work conditions.

But when I gained the confidence of these workers, I then understood the complete reality. What they contested, what they would not tolerate was the very lifestyle of which they knew themselves to be victims. Summarizing it by the "subway-job-sleep" formula, they declared:

> You think that this is a life, this? . . . Getting up solely to be attached to a machine that transforms me into a cog, then to return exhausted to stuff myself, like an ass, and sprawl myself on my straw mattress? . . . Even to make love, impossible! Too tired . . . There's not only the wage, the work conditions. We must have a different society, you get it? . . . Another one where nobody should be reduced to a screw in a machine. And if, to obtain it, we need, like you yourself say, the revolution, OK, agreed! If messing

things up can serve to create justice, then long live the mess! . . . What's there to lose from this, for us, the proletarians, if not a life of poverty? . . . So, if, like you say, "under the pavement, the beach," I'm ready to de-pave all of France to enjoy this beach, like all the others.

I, like many of my comrades, did not limit myself to the status of student. I was perfectly aware that it was provisional; it prepared and influenced my future as citizen, as adult: either on the side of rulers/exploiters or on the side of the slaves. Thus, my student status was animated by the future citizen that I would become. For myself and my comrades, it was quite obvious. We declared it explicitly from the beginning and had acted according to our intentions. Our essential concern was not to study to find a profession. From the beginning and especially, our concern was action aimed at establishing a new society where studies were directed not to rejoin the herd of wage slaves or the class of privileged exploiters, but to construct a life in harmony with oneself, with every human being and with nature in which we live.

All these aspects my comrades and I discussed together, but henceforth with death in our souls. We very much felt that the incoming tide had run dry. We now had to face the horrible ebb.

21

Harvests: The "Spirit of May"

Nevertheless, my life in this golden period produced seeds that gave beautiful harvests. Concerning myself personally, it seems useful briefly to present them here.[1]

Toward the end of July 1968, I decided to return to the "countryside" of the planet, in the dominated "Third World" according to Maoist theory (or the "periphery" according to others), to pursue the liberation struggle; this would lead to the struggle in the "cities" (or the "center"), the dominating developed countries.

My choice was triggered by a particular reason. Under various pretexts, judicial proceedings had begun against more or less important leaders of the movement. Already, on July 10, militants of the extreme left, Alain Krivine among them, were arrested and imprisoned.[2] Other comrades suffered the same fate. I was informed that the police were searching especially for foreigners who participated in the movement. I was one of these, and one of the worst, being Algerian. My actions, however modest, were not completely anonymous.

I did not want to see myself reduced to inaction in a prison, with the risk of a "blunder," more easily carried out on a *basané*, then to be expelled from the country and banned from returning because of "subversive activities."

---

1. Most of these are presented in detail in my book, *Ethique et esthétique au théâtre et alentours*, http://www.kadour-naimi.com/f-ecrits_theatre.html.

2. Trotskyist leader Alain Krivine was a prominent spokesperson during May and June 1968 as the founder of the JCR (Revolutionary Communist Youth).

I therefore chose to return to my land of birth, Algeria. Not from nationalism, but simply because the people living there were those I knew best. It was there that I could continue my liberation activity.

I left France at the beginning of August. Since my financial means were limited, I traveled among emigrant workers who returned by boat to see their families.

At the end of the month, in Oran, I created a self-managed theatrical company: the Theatre of the Sea: Company of Research and Experimental Theatrical Productions. Of notice was the emphasis placed on *research* and *experimentation*. The troupe was autonomous at the same time that all professional theater was subordinate to the state dictatorship of an army colonel.

The company functioned in a self-managed manner, the content of works aimed at social liberation, and aesthetics gave priority to innovative research. The audience was primarily workers of town and countryside, as well as university students, lycée students, and enlightened intellectuals. Spectators were encouraged to intervene during rehearsals as well as performances. The latter would conclude with a debate. In Algeria of that time, suffering under military rule, such discussion allowed a certain freedom of expression that was otherwise forbidden.

The play and discussion took place in a circular form, even on the ground, just like the assemblies of May–June 1968 and like traditional grassroots Algerian plays on public squares. In the photo on the next page, the performance of *La Valeur de l'Accord* (The Value of Agreement, 1969) took place in the courtyard of the Bouchaoui self-managed farm in the presence of peasants and students. In the middle, with my back to the camera, I presented the play.

Two years later, the Ministry of Labor and Social Affairs agreed to finance the troupe on condition that we continue our theatrical activity, now enlarged to include cultural organizing, within professional training centers. Thus, the troupe operated principally at the service of young future manual workers and technicians of industry and agriculture. Excellent situation!

At this time, I had theorized the notion of *alter-*, *co-*, and *auto*-theater. This last practice, authentically self-managed, encouraged autonomous action by the young workers themselves.

a valeur de l'accord

The experience lasted about three years, from the end of August 1968 to the beginning of 1972.

The end of the company was caused, on the one hand, by pressure from state authorities upset by our activity and, on the other, by "critical support" given to them by "socialists" and a well-known intellectual Stalinist in the country. In a French newspaper, without having the courage to give my name, he reproached me for my "leftism" and spoke of "youth who have everything save having lived."[3] It was an indirect way of attacking, through my person, the May–June social movement in France.

I observed with disgust that clichés about that movement and its participants continued to serve as excuses to hide compromises of principles, even beyond France.

3. Remarks by Kateb Yacine, reported by Colette Godard, *Le Monde*, September 11, 1975. Kateb Yacine was a well-known Algerian writer and member of the Algerian Communist Party.

I concerned myself with workers at the Institute of Professional Training, which was dependent on the Ministry of Labor. I succeeded in organizing, guiding, and teaching within the framework of a training program for a group of future cultural organizers. Discretely, they had access to knowledge allowing them to self-manage their own cultural activities in order to do so later themselves among young workers.

At the same time, the institute workers elected me to be secretary of the base-level union section. Contrary to the statutes of the exclusive trade union (UGTA, the General Union of Algerian Workers), a "transmission belt" of the state, I adopted a self-management approach. It is interesting to know how this was done.

While the previous union representative, complicit with the hierarchy, never held worker assemblies, I organized these regularly each month. During the meeting, I contented myself with acting most strictly as only a "secretary." On the left page of a notebook, I wrote down the demands of the workers. Then I went to the institute director and asked him to respond to the workers on the righthand page. But difficulties arose as soon as the first meeting with this "progressive" bureaucrat.

At the next monthly assembly, I communicated his rejections. I then wrote down new demands of the workers that I then presented again to the director. His responses were evasive.

This game lasted close to a year. At the end of that time, the union hierarchy sent me a letter in which, arbitrarily, they dismissed me from my position because of unacceptable "agitation." Several days later, while denouncing my "anarchist" action, the institute director demanded my transfer to a professional training center. I preferred to resign from the institute.

Returning to Oran, the city where my family resided, I resumed my social studies. I wished to complete the education acquired during the months of May, June, and July 1968. A passing anecdote: I wanted to carry out my studies in the quite small shoe workshop of my father, at that time unoccupied. Seeing the work instruments and smelling the odors of leather inspired me by putting me in contact physically, not only symbolically, with the world of labor. I wanted to learn more about social self-management.

In 1973, the director of the Regional State Theatre of Oran offered me a collaborative project. He suggested that I write a piece on the "Socialist Management of Enterprises," a reform launched by the military dictatorship state while masking its action with the "socialist" label. I asked the director to approve my research in factories across the whole country, from the very largest to the very smallest, so I could know what I would write about. In this way, I could learn the true reality of the workers. I received his consent.

During one whole month, I visited enterprises. With assistance from comrades, I succeeded in contacting trade unionists truly representative of the workers and observing work conditions. What enrichment through understanding the proletariat, even though I was the son of a worker! And what indignation, on viewing the repugnant economic exploitation and cruel political domination of which they were victims! And with the complicity of the union and the regime.

This month in the field was a valuable practical lesson. I understood, among other things, that so-called socialist management aimed in reality at two goals. On the one hand, it tried to definitively eliminate whatever remained of self-management in the enterprises, which had been established spontaneously by workers just after independence to compensate for the flight of colonial bosses. On the other, it sought to establish a state capitalism allowing the ruling class to consolidate itself as a statist bourgeoisie.

Upon return to the regional theater, I refused to write a work on the theme of that reform, knowing the impossibility of telling the truth.

The director then suggested to me that I compose a piece for "children." I proposed to do so. It praised the freedom of a family of "wolves." They preferred the harsh difficulties of their life for love of their autonomy and despised the existence of "dogs," who benefited from material comfort but at the price of servitude. The work was refused by the "reader committee" of the state theater, which was composed of "progressives"—in other words, Marxists of the PAGS (the Party of the Socialist Avant-Garde, formerly the Algerian Communist Party). The reason given for its rejection: the text was contrary to the ideas children had about wolves and dogs.

In Algeria, I felt no longer able to act by my convictions. My "1968 leftism" was known. The local "communists" of the PAGS denounced it, almost publicly.

This made it easier for authorities to use against me the classic treatment reserved for radical opponents: "to disappear" without leaving a trace, to be a victim of a driving "accident" or another "unexpected" and "mysterious" event.

I left for Belgium at the end of 1973.

Once again, concerned with improving my theoretical education and historical knowledge, I chose the Catholic University of Louvain and not the *Free* University of Brussels for one precise reason. In the former, managed by Jesuits, the teaching was more free than that in the second institution—where Marxists ruled.

On the basis of material gathered during my research among Algerian enterprises, I wrote a bachelor's thesis. It showed the duplicity of the so-called socialist reform. That measure definitively eliminated worker and peasant self-management, to the gain of a state capitalism, consolidating a bourgeoisie of the same nature.[4]

Following this, I began a research doctorate, the title of which was "Transformation of Revolutionary Ruptures into Totalitarian Conservative Systems: The Cases of Russia and Algeria."[5]

I needed to understand these failed processes. Perhaps, in a certain way, they would help me to better clarify that of May–June 1968.

During my investigations, I had, finally, studied seriously the writings of the first anarchist militants and theorists: Proudhon, Bakunin, James Guillaume, Malatesta, Pierre Kropotkin, Voline, Emma Goldman, and so forth. Thus, I better assessed the Marxists, beginning with their founder, followed by Lenin, Trotsky, Mao Zedong, Fidel Castro, Che Guevara, and so on.

4. Kadour Naïmi, "La reforme de l'entreprise en algerie" (Bachelor's thesis, Université catholique de Louvain, 1979), https://bib.uclouvain.be/opac/ucl/fr/chamo/chamo:683489?i=0#.

5. The presentation can be viewed at http://www.kadour-naimi.com/f-societe-autogestion-heterogestion-revolution.htm. The introductory theoretical section was published in Italian in *Invarianti*, an Italian trimonthly politicocultural revue (published by Antonio Pellicani Editeur in Rome), in three parts: vol. 2, no. 7 (Autumn 1988); vol. 3, no. 8 (Winter 1988–1989); and vol. 3, nos. 9/10 (Spring-Summer 1989).

Once having gained the clarity I needed, I gave up on presenting a thesis. A university career did not interest me. I was quite doubtful about positive pedagogical activity within the university. The great majority of students were obsessed solely with becoming mandarins comfortably paid by the ruling classes.

Among young Belgians in 1980, the May–June 1968 movement was ignored or "passed by." Already, I was viewed as an "ancient combatant" who would do better to speak of something else, of the present and not what he lived through, which was of no current relevance and now useless.

Nevertheless, I participated in a militant group without labels with a self-management tendency. This led me to offer "critical support" to actions of the German RAF.[6] In the extreme-left weekly *Pour la révolution*, I published a poem on this subject, signed with a pseudonym, to avoid worries about eventual tendentious accusations of "supporting terrorism."[7]

In 1982, I sought direct contact with so-called ordinary people by resuming artistic activity. I emigrated to the country of "neorealist" cinema, Italy, moving to Rome.

I involved myself in theater and film productions. They were destined for working people and for concerned intellectuals. Of course, these works were marginal compared with the dominant bourgeois system, as well as its "progressive" allies and subordinates.

Finally, I created a small independent production house for films and documentaries: Maldoror Film. Its principle: ethics at the service of aesthetics. A few works were produced.

I also founded both the International Festival of Free Theatre and the International Festival of Free Cinema. These initiatives were autonomous, voluntary, and run by self-management principles. Their goal: to encourage those authors opposed to the dominant system to meet each other, to unite them in order to create a free countersystem with solidarity. At the end of three years, it became evident that these artists, aged from twenty to about forty,

6. The German Red Army Faction.
7. The text and audio version are available at http://www.litteratureaudio .com/livre-audio-gratuit-mp3/naimi-kadour-cing-doigts-de-la-main-arraches-poeme.html.

gained from these festivals by presenting their productions, but they showed no interest in a union aimed at alternative production in freedom and solidarity. Their appearance at the festivals seemed motivated solely by concern to become known in order to gain access to the dominant system.

Parallel to this, I visited the *centri sociali autogestiti* (self-managed social centers). I wanted to know how much the "spirit of May" existed there and in what forms.

But I had the air of an "old combatant" among most of the young people who surrounded me. Perhaps they considered me a "loser" who had nothing to teach them. Nevertheless, I tried to contribute to this grassroots movement by seeking to understand the desires of these new companions while avoiding any paternalist attitude on my part.

I also wanted to know why, in certain self-managed centers, there were too few persons of my age—a ridiculously low and insignificant number. Was it that now we found ourselves no longer having a place, for a stupidly biological reason, or because we were the vanquished? Was it because others abandoned the struggle for reasons of marriage, of forming a family, of "career," or of something else?

In 1982, on return to Strasbourg for a brief visit, I had two significant meetings.

I saw an ex-comrade of Moroccan origin. He had greatly assisted me at the beginning of my Marxist theoretical education. Having become a psychiatrist, he received me in his quite comfortable home. From the rather conventional and cold discussion, I understood his thinking. He had successfully gone beyond his "juvenile utopian phase of enthusiasm." Here he was, living "as he should, as a realistic adult," whereas for me . . . These accounts implied that I was a "failure," having never gone beyond my Peter Pan stage.

I recalled that the "participation" of this ex-comrade in the movement consisted of following it from a distance while commenting about it like a Marxist-Leninist Maoist. Perhaps, holding a comfortable scholarship from the government of his country, he feared that active militancy with us would lead it to be withdrawn.

By contrast, another Maoist ex-comrade, Jean, nicknamed Nigro, became a union militant at the university. He pursued his path, always animated by "our 1968 spirit." We were very happy to see each other again and to observe that we had kept and continued to practice the same ideals.

Another source of happiness is the memory of exceptional human beings I knew during the months of May and June 1968: Jean "Nigro," Laurent, Edith, Bakou, David, D* . . . and so many other students, workers, citizens whose names but not faces I've forgotten. They remain as "guardian angels" who accompany my existence, lively flames in the surrounding darkness.

During and after the U.S. aggression against Iraq in 2003, I wrote a voluminous essay, *La guerre, pourquoi? la paix, comment: Eléments de discussion pour gens de bonne volonté.*[8] As the subtitle indicates, the essay is directed to so-called ordinary people. My relations with persons in my neighborhood, simple citizens, showed me the need to address myself to them while placing at their disposal information that had been hidden as much by the dominant Italian media as by those of the "progressive" opposition.

The work criticizes the statist hierarchical organization of societies in general; it concludes with the need for generalized social self-management as the true solution to ending war between nations, a consequence of war between social classes.

In 2012, I returned to Algeria where I agreed to produce a play, *La tendresse, les enfants!* (Tenderness, the Children), in the context of an international theater festival. The theme: an elegy for independent and free thinking in solidarity, guaranteed by nonviolent resistance against the totalitarian, hierarchical, violent, and fascist mentality.

Since then, I've dedicated myself to the regular publication of columns in an independent online newspaper, *Le Matin d'Algérie.* The goal: to make known and to defend social self-management as an alternative practice to the bankruptcy of "liberalism" and of "Marxism," without forgetting the fascism of religious or ethnic expression.

8. The title in English is *War, Why? Peace, How: Elements of Discussion for People of Good Will.* The essay is available at http://www.kadour-naimi.com/f_sociologie_ ecrits.html.

My realism still searches for what seems impossible. A utopia is only considered utopian because of the lack of conditions for its achievement.

Otherwise, what's the use of living? In this present period of the people's regression and of the ferocity of rulers under capitalist globalization, the spirit of May lives on!

January 2018

Postface

Several final general observations on the May 1968 movement in France: It broke out at the same time that the best-known "experts" described the "lethargy" of the people. Why then could not a more or less similar movement surge forth once again? Humanity is a succession of generations, including liberating flood tides and enslaving ebb tides. Nevertheless, it is false to declare that there is "nothing new under the sun." Since the revolt of the enslaved in the "West," led by Spartacus, and ancient peasant revolts in the "East," humanity has progressed all the way to the present, despite everything. Why could it not continue?

If the barbarous instinct of domination-exploitation endures, presenting itself under different heads of a same hydra, is it rational to believe that the opposite instinct, of freedom in solidarity, doesn't persist in manifesting itself in diverse forms?

The experience of living the most beautiful moments of individual and collective happiness leaves people with an intense desire to enjoy it once again, in one way or another. If the opportunity doesn't present itself, such people try hard nevertheless to contribute to it, according to their personal capacities and social circumstances. The essential thing is not to resign oneself but to act in the direction of equity, even if one is reduced to the most humble and apparently insignificant gestures. Drops of water can become a stream, and then a river, according to the social "temperature."

Within the "ashes" of the May–June 1968 movement, sparks twinkle from time to time. In France in 2016, for example, the "Nuit Debout" phenomenon ("Rise Up at Night" protests) recalled the feverish nights of study and discussion in May 1968. In 1989, once again in springtime, more precisely in April, May, and June, didn't the Tiananmen Square movement abroad in Beijing benefit from the breeze of the "1968 spirit"? And, finally, didn't the grass-roots revolts in Arab countries recall the "spirit of May"?

If one attempts to define it in the briefest manner, that spirit resides in the fundamental challenge to every authoritarian mentality, whatever its form. Of course, by "authority" I mean that which aims to dominate so as to exploit human beings. If I had to write a history of May–June 1968 in France, I would commence with this phrase: "At the beginning as at the end was: *No to enslaving authority!*" And I would make clear: "The partisans of this revolt were essentially peaceable. From whence came their greatness and . . . their weakness."

In the end, in my opinion, this aspect—*freedom in solidarity against exploitive authority*—separated partisans and enemies of the "spirit of May": hope of a new liberating tide in the former, fear in the latter. What was able to happen before could surge forth again, in other forms, conforming more to current realities. Perhaps it would emerge at an improvised moment as usual, and with surprise, to the extent that a chief of state is forced to abandon his base of power. Let us only hope that, in what follows, the liberating movement finds the means to endure, to strengthen itself and to become a positive inspiration for other peoples.

In the present context, the new planetary enemy of "world terrorism," after the fall of the "Communist bloc," appears at just the right moment to instill fear among citizens and to justify every measure of surveillance and domination by the planetary state elites. They are obsessed with banishing a democratic citizenry that contests a system proclaiming itself as the economic and political "model" of reference, the ideal "civilization" and the "end of history." But the dogma of Margaret Thatcher that "there is no alternative" is put in doubt. Proposals as well as political and social experiences have appeared, searching for acceptable alternatives. The people have not offered their final word as to freedom and solidarity.

AK Press is small, in terms of staff and resources, but we also manage to be one of the world's most productive anarchist publishing houses. We publish close to twenty books every year, and distribute thousands of other titles published by like-minded independent presses and projects from around the globe. We're entirely worker-run and democratically managed. We operate without a corporate structure—no boss, no managers, no bullshit.

The Friends of AK program is a way you can directly contribute to the continued existence of AK Press, and ensure that we're able to keep publishing books like this one! Friends pay $25 a month directly into our publishing account ($30 for Canada, $35 for international), and receive a copy of every book AK Press publishes for the duration of their membership! Friends also receive a discount on anything they order from our website or buy at a table: 50% on AK titles, and 20% on everything else. We have a Friends of AK ebook program as well: $15 a month gets you an electronic copy of every book we publish for the duration of your membership. You can even sponsor a very discounted membership for someone in prison.

Email friendsofak@akpress.org for more info, or visit the Friends of
   AK Press website: https://www.akpress.org/friends.html

There are always great book projects in the works—so sign up now to
   become a Friend of AK Press, and let the presses roll!